M000076047

FEB 18 2013

Kalaupapa, HI

MY NAME IS
Makia

My Name Is
Makia
A Memoir of Kalaupapa

by Makia Malo

with Pamela Young

WATERMARK
PUBLISHING

© 2011 Inka Blue LLC

All rights reserved. No part of this book may be reproduced in
any form or by any electronic or mechanical means, including
information retrieval systems, without prior written permission
from the publisher, except for brief passages quoted in reviews.

ISBN 978-1-935690-29-0

Library of Congress Control Number: 2012943872

Design and production
Gonzalez Design Company

Front cover photos
Gary Sprinkle (Makia Malo), courtesy Yodie Noe Mizukami (family),
Richard Miller (house), Hawai'i State Department of Health (admis-
sion photo), Franco Salmoiraghi/Photo Resource Hawai'i (cover
background and title pages)

Back cover photo
Gary Sprinkle

Watermark Publishing
1088 Bishop Street, Suite 310
Honolulu, Hawai'i 96813
Telephone 1-808-587-7766
Toll-free 1-866-900-BOOK
sales@bookshawaii.net
www.bookshawaii.net

Printed in the United States

Contents

*Dedicated to all those
who came to Kalaupapa before me*

-Makia Malo

Introduction

The great thing is, if one can, to stop regarding all the unpleasant things as interruptions in one's "own" or "real" life. The truth is, of course, that what one regards as interruptions are precisely one's life.
—C.S. Lewis

As a child, Elroy Makia Malo never had to ponder the vagaries of fate. His future was decided for him. His life would not be vastly different from his father's, or his father's before him. The barefoot boy from Papakōlea would grow taro and perhaps learn a trade in postwar Honolulu.

But Makia loved learning, and through his hidden passion for books he began to see his future differently. Through a series of minor miracles he found himself a university graduate, then a university instructor, then an internationally acclaimed storyteller. But the price was high.

At the age of twelve, Makia contracted leprosy, now called Hansen's disease. He, two brothers, a sister and eventually his mother were diagnosed with what was then called *maʻi Pākē*, the Chinese illness, or *maʻi hoʻokaʻawale ʻohana*, the sickness that tears families apart.

Beginning in 1865, leprosy patients in Hawaiʻi were exiled to the Makanalua peninsula on the island of Molokaʻi. The first settlement was at Kalawao, where thousands of the afflicted struggled to survive with inconsistent supplies of food and medicine. By the time Makia was sent away (1947), the settlement had moved farther inland to Kalaupapa. The government, charitable organizations, and churches had set up dormitories and clinics. Sulfone drugs successfully arrested the disease for most patients. Makia was not one of them. The disease would eventually claim his hands, feet, and eyesight. But his mind remained sharp, holding on to childhood memories, and filing away the details of his new adventures in Kalaupapa. These became his tickets around the world as a "scald"— a teller of tales, a poet with passionate stories of innocence, love, and horror. And through this oral history we walk through a painful part of Hawaiʻi's past.

The following pages are gleaned from conversations with Makia over nearly three years. Between chapters are transcriptions of the actual stories he has shared with audiences. The reader will notice several styles of speech. When Makia is reminiscing about his early years in Papakōlea, he slips into the patois of his youth. His university days are recalled in near-perfect standard English. Later, some of his stories were edited by his wife, Ann. Most of the conversations are in pidgin, standard English, or a combination of both.

Makia and the other seventeen remaining Kalaupapa patients have been interviewed and quoted many times. There is a tendency for writers to correct their broken grammar. I promised Makia I would not. The perceived errors in speech and syntax are part of pidgin communication, and since Makia has proven himself a master of the spoken word, who am I to alter the language?

This book is the result of a simple request Makia made following the canonization of Father Damien in 2009. I was part of the Hawaiʻi media delegation to the Vatican. "Saint Damien: A Man Called Kamiano" was a news special I produced, documenting thirty years of coverage in Kalaupapa, Belgium, and Rome. Makia asked me for a DVD to give to his niece Noe "so I can leave her something after I go." I suggested she would be much happier with her uncle's memoirs. And so began our weekly meetings at Hale Mōhalu hospital in Kaimukī.

Having grown up with a blind sister who was also confined to a wheelchair, I was never uncomfortable with Makia's disabilities. In fact we often shared that strange nonverbal communication that passes between members of a disabled household. He seemed happiest when remembering his brother Pilipili and the camaraderie of hunting pals in the Kalaupapa mountains. Some of his stories are myths, some are daydreams, with no beginning, end, or purpose.

A note about the word "leprosy": Many patients refuse to acknowledge the word because of the biblical stigma. They refer to themselves as Hansen's disease patients. I have found that the sensitivities are largely regional. Patients I spoke to from Mother Teresa's Calcutta Leprosarium call themselves lepers. A patient from Carville, Louisiana, chastised me for saying "Hansen's disease" because "leprosy is the word Jesus used." Makia uses both, but most often "leprosy." If the use of the word is objectionable to the reader, no offense is intended.

—*Pamela Young*

Chapter One

The first time I heard the word "leprosy" was at church. We were taught that only sinners got leprosy. Maybe that's why we never talked about it, even after my brother Bill was sent away. I never knew it was in my family until I was sent to Kalaupapa myself. After Bill, my kid brother Pilipili got it. Then my sister Beka. She had to leave behind a husband and two kids. Then me. My brother David I didn't know very well because at seventeen he joined the merchant marine, then the Navy. I think that's why he never got the disease.

I had three other brothers: George I, who died, George II, and Stanley, who at the age of sixteen died when he fell off the Papakōlea bridge. My sister Margaret died at the age of one. Nine altogether. I am the last one alive. I sometimes wonder why. I think it's because I have a story to tell.

I remember one day Mama telling Pili, "Pilipili, you put on this sweater and don't take it off." His arm was disfigured, the skin swollen already. As far back as I can remember it seemed Pili always had the signs, even as a young boy. Mama said, "Don't remove that sweater, you hear me?" And Pili looked at Mama and looked down at his arm. "Yeah, okay, Mama."

At Pauoa Elementary School we used to have lot of *lehua* plants. Us boys used to go and catch honeybees. Once the honeybee gets into the *lehua* blossom, drink the nectar, they drunk. They don't attack. So you can reach slowly and grab the honeybee by the wings and hold 'em like that. And they bend their *'ōkole* up, you know, try sting anything. What we did, we get one leather belt and we rub the *'ōkole* of the honeybee onto the belt and the bee would sting the belt. And the stinger come out. Then we go put the bees on our face, put 'em on our hand, we go by the girls, "Look!" and frighten the girls, stuff like that.

So one day I was looking by this plant, you know, watching this honeybee. Pili was right next to me and then I hear this voice say, "Earl, what's that on your arm?" Earl was Pili's English name. The second-grade teacher, Mrs. Ho, was standing over him. Pili had taken off his sweater.

Pretty soon after, Mama took Pilipili and me to the movies. It was *They Died with Their Boots On* with Errol Flynn. Afterward we went for ice cream. Funny how you can remember the little details. I remember this day so clear because that was the last day Pili and I spent together before he went away.

The next morning we wake up and Mama and Daddy say we going for a ride. Okay, so the four of us in the car, Mama and Daddy in front, Pili and me sitting in the back of that old '36 Chevy. We stopped in front of this long building and Daddy tells Pili to get out of the car and stay on the side of the road and wait. We didn't know what was going on, but Pili went. There was a man sitting on the porch of the building looking at us. Mama says, "You stand there and don't move, you hear me?" Pili just nodded, the way he always did when Mama scolded him. Then I heard the trunk close. Daddy had gotten out a suitcase. He put it next to Pili. Then Daddy got in the car and we drove away. I remember I'm on my knees looking back out the rear window and seeing Pili crying. He looked to the sky and just cried. I could see his tears as we drove away and he got smaller and smaller in the window. I cried out, "Pili! Pili!" Then the man on the porch got out of his chair and walked up to Pili. He put his arm around my brother and led him into the building.

At home my mother was crying but I couldn't ask 'cause I didn't want get lickin's. We just didn't talk about it. That's the way it was. Some things you just didn't talk about. I didn't know that Pili was the second child in the family to get the disease. And no one could have known then that there would be another, then another.

The next time we saw Pili was a week later. We went to visit him at Kalihi Hospital. I was so excited. There was a fence around the whole compound. You drive in the front gate, the road to the right went to the hospital and there's a little shack. A patient was hired to sit there in case any visitors came. Today it was a *haole* girl. She asked who we came to see and we said, "Earl Malo." Then she went to look for him. My kid brother didn't come out right away so we waited and waited. And then I look way down and I see this action going on, like two people running around. As they got closer I could see it was my kid brother and another *haole* girl. She was trying to hug him but he would get away and take off and she chased him. She was all smiles. Her nickname was Blondie.

The fence was about four feet tall, a double fence, about eight feet between, filled with plants, trimmed to the level of the gate. You couldn't pass anything over. You could throw in something to eat, but they couldn't throw anything out to you. Mother McLaren was the head at the time. I was so happy to see Pili. We were always together and I was so lonely without him.

My parents were solemn, but seeing he was okay, they felt better. Other people came and sat on the benches to visit family members. That was the routine, just like prison. Pili stayed in the hospital for a year and then it was time to send him to Kalaupapa. I remember we went down to the docks and saw him off on the boat. He had the red bumps by then.

Next to get the disease was my older sister Pearl, who we called Beka. Her Hawaiian name was Keali'i'ilikapeka, which means Queen Elizabeth. For short we called her Beka. She was married and her husband went off to the service. In many ways she was our mother since my parents worked from early morning to evening. She got turned in to the Health Department by her husband. See, there was this Norwegian family in Papakōlea. They didn't really fit in but they bother nobody and they had this son, who we called Boy. I don't know his real name. Anyway Beka married Boy Olsen and they had a daughter, Olga. But when Boy went off to fight in the war Beka went help out at the USO and she got to know the servicemen. She got pregnant and so Boy left her.

One day I'm in the yard picking cherries and Daddy looks up and starts cursing. We see Boy on the bridge looking at us. When it was time for Beka to go Kalaupapa on the boat, Boy was on the pier. He was crying. I think he still loved her. After that I found myself in charge of the girls, her two daughters, Olga and Tweetie.

When one person has it in the family, the government keeps track. Leprosy was feared by everyone, so everybody on the lookout. I was too young to understand. I didn't even know what signs to look for, at least not until it was too late.

We used to climb up from under Papakōlea bridge to the road. There was a pipe that went up the rail about fifteen feet up. This place, I don't know if they were using for garbage dump or something, but there were a lot of broken bottles. I cut my foot because we go barefoot, yeah? Ah shucks. My feet had lost feeling already. That was a sign, I learned later. I'd had other signs before. My teacher at Pauoa would ask me why my eyes were so red and I told her, "Because I go swimming a lot."

Up by Papakōlea bridge there was a lot of gravels because they were building the road up there. My foot was so sore I told my Dad. Daddy was working taro patch, using poison spray to kill the grass, so he had these raw wounds on both legs. The chemicals started eating up at his legs, so when he came home he would soak his feet in warm water and spray Lysol every day. So that's what I did. We had a Chinese table, the kind with two chairs on either side facing each other. He said, "You sit there, put your foot on top." He took his knife and scraped my foot. All of a sudden something pop out. It was one of those black gravels. Then he dressed my leg. Even with the numbness it hurt.

We had this medicine we put on almost everything, this yellow powder. Mama would make it damp and scoop it out and put it on the wounds. Some places on my legs were numb, some very sensitive. I realized that when I'd stepped on that glass it didn't hurt the way it should have.

"Son, tomorrow you not going school," my Daddy says one day.

"Oh yeah, how come, Daddy?"

"We going see docta' tomorrow."

"Docta' fo' what?"

"Neva' mind, questions, questions."

We're not sure who turned us in. Maybe Boy. He had a real grudge against the family. The next morning we show up at Dr. Edwin Chung Hoon's office. He had a razor and he nicked my ear for a little specimen, you know, some blood from the wound. Then he did the same to my Daddy. Two hours later he came out. He said, "Mr. Malo, I have good news. You don't have the disease. But I'm afraid your son Elroy does. He has to go to Kalihi Hospital." That was Friday, September 27, 1947.

I can't imagine what Daddy thought. Another kid, oh geez. He says, "I no like my boy go Kalihi. I like my boy go straight to Kalaupapa today, you know, with his brothers and sistah."

The doctor explains cannot today because the plane went already. Another plane in one week. By this time the patients didn't go by boat anymore. In 1947, the airline started flying to Kalaupapa every Friday. Why did Daddy want me go? I think he thought it would be easier on Mama. He didn't want to see her cry anymore.

Of course, back home, nothing was said to me. I had my suspicions but I didn't ask what it all meant. That week I neva' went school. Then nine o'clock in the morning the phone rings.

"Hello, Elroy." Oh, I recognize the voice. Vice principal Okazaki.

"How come you're not in school today?" Oh, I was so flustered. I was searching my mind what to say. I didn't want to lie.

"Oh, I sick."

"Well then, perhaps tomorrow you'll come to school."

"Oh yeah, yeah."

The rest of the day I worried about what the heck he went call fo'. That evening Mama and Daddy coming up the driveway. I'm running alongside the car.

"Mama, you know the man from school called."

"What did you say?"

"I told him I was sick."

"Well, tomorrow if he calls back you tell him to call Docta' Chung Hoon."

And so, same thing early the next morning the telephone rings.

"Hello, Elroy, how come you're not in school again today?"

"Oh, you know, Mr. Okazaki, my Mama says fo' you call Docta' Chung Hoon."

There's this silence. Then he says, "Oh, okay," and he hangs up. Not until years later did I realize that when he hung up that phone a part of my life was over. I would neva' go back school, neva' see my friends again.

The following Friday my parents drove me to the airport. My cousin Joe was with me, Auntie Jessie, and one of Mama's friends, Betty Aki. Joe and I went into the hangar at Andrew's Flying Service, 'cause you know, we *nīele*. We started looking around. Then I heard a noise and saw a Health Department station wagon pull in, two guys get out and then two kids with the father of one of them. "What's going to happen?" I said to myself. Then they said time to get on board. Mama was crying, no words, just kissing me, hugging me. Everybody came to hug me. My Daddy is sniffling. Mama kissing me and whispered only for my ears, she says, "Oh, Lord, why me?" So I say, "Mama, no cry. I going be okay." Then I turned around and walked to the plane. ❧

Chapter Two

We took off, the pilot and the father up front, the three boys in the back. I was on the left-hand side. In the middle was Small Henry (Leong), who was only eight years old, and on the other side was Heed (Silva). I looked at Heed and thought, "Oh, my God." I went to school with him at Pauoa in Papakōlea. I remember he just disappeared and I wondered what happened to him. Now I knew. I tried to get his attention but he just looked away.

Nobody talked in the plane. As we went down the runway I tried to look back to see Mama and Daddy for the last time but my seat was too low and I couldn't see them.

Later on we stretch and look out the window and see what we were leaving, Waikīkī, Diamond Head, and the point beyond. We saw Oʻahu end.

We scared, yeah? But still to me it was an adventure. After awhile we could see Molokaʻi on the right side. It was all *pali* and I asked myself, "What kind place this?" And we fly along the *pali*, these straight cliffs that went on and on forever.

We landed at the Kalaupapa airstrip and I remember seeing this long row of cars along the low fence. A lot of them were jalopies. You know, the salt air eats up the body of the car, and so they'd just tear the parts off and use lumber to build up the car.

A station wagon pulls up with Mr. Lawrence Judd, who was the superintendent at the time. The two boys, the father, and the pilot went with him. I was left all by myself under a tree. I was told to wait there until my sister picked me up. She was working in the dining room and it was lunchtime so she couldn't get off early. So for an hour I looked at the mountains, the ocean. It was so beautiful. This was six days before my thirteenth birthday.

Then I saw all these people by the hangar looking at me. They had handkerchiefs around their necks and over their faces. I didn't know that underneath they were hiding damaged noses and the trachea tubes that helped them breathe. I just remember thinking, "Wow, this place get plenty cowboys."

And then I hear a car pull up and someone yelling, "'Kia! 'Kia!" I jumped up and saw my sister in an orange jalopy with no doors. I called out, "Beka!" and started running. But then this other kid is coming toward me and I almost didn't recognize him. It was Pilipili, my younger brother. He didn't look like how I remembered him. His face was swollen and had sores. His nose damaged, both hands swollen. I was surprised, but he was my brother. We all hugged and kissed, I was so happy to be with family. The tears came down my face. Beka, she hug me and wipe away my tears saying, "No cry, Makia, everything is all right." I just hug her back saying, "Beka, Beka." And then I say, "Mama."

The guy behind my sister was her boyfriend, Johnny Aruda. They got married the next year. We drove across one wooden bridge, then zigzag to a hill. Then I see Baldwin Home where Heed and Small Henry was taken. Then we turn left and pass the hospital. Beka says, "You come here Monday to see the docta'." Pili was actually staying in the hospital but Beka asked the nurses if he could come home, stay with me for one night so I not so scared.

We drove past the store, called Kalaupapa Board Store, past the Catholic church, past Katie's Store, and Tomita's Store, the other side, past the bakery, the post office.

"This is the meat house and the ice house," Beka says. "This is where Pu'a works." That was the Hawaiian name for my older brother Bill. "Pu'a! Pu'a!" she calls. He didn't come out right away so Johnny went in the back, look for him. It was then Pu'a comes sauntering out of the office.

"Hi, Makia. How are you?"

"Fine." I didn't notice I was reading his lips. He had no voice. With his mouth moving and the hisses and clicks and clacks of his tongue I could make out what he was saying. He had a tube in his throat. I remember years ago Mama got a letter from Bill. He said he was having trouble breathing because his throat was closing up, so they put in a tube. At the time I thought, "This guy my bruddah? I don't even know what he looks like." I thought, "Oh, God, a tube in his throat? What happens when it rains?" I thought maybe he would drown, ha! That's the way kids think.

We drove to Beka's cottage, which had a living room, a kitchen and three bedrooms. My sister was in one, Bill in one, Pili and me in one. The cottage was part of a housing compound that made up the McVeigh Home, which was for families and single adults. The Baldwin Home was for boys, the Bishop Home for girls, all kine of like dormitories, where the patients slept and ate, three meals a day. There was another compound for the patients that were really sick.

Everything was provided by the government. Medical care, too. Not like the old days when the first patients had to fight over food and build their own shelter out of bits of lumber and palm fronds. If you lived outside the dormitories, like us, you'd get a regular food ration each week. Ten dollars at the store. Every other week the *kōkuas* (nonpatient helpers, often relatives of settlement residents) would slaughter cattle and hand out the meat.

Later on, Pili and Beka showed me around. My sister tried to prepare me.

She said, "Don't be too *niele*, don't ask questions. They're embarrassed about themselves, what they look like." So once again I found myself in a place where no one wanted to talk about it.

In the McVeigh dining room I thought, "Jus' like one restaurant." Lots of tables, each one four chairs. This is where we would be eating if we not cooking at home. Since Beka worked in the dining room as a waitress, she ate with the workers so I sit with Pili, Bill, and Johnny. The waitresses were all patients. The cooks were *kōkuas*.

So the way it works is the waitress brings out the food in a bowl with one fork, spoon, and napkin. On the table is shoyu, sugar and our daily medication. You want more fo' eat, you tap your plate. I was embarrassed first time, but later I felt grown up! Jus' like one restaurant. The napkins were paper, not like the cut-up rice bag we had at home.

The whole time we eating, people looking at our table. You know how sometimes you know people looking, looking at you, you get real *lōlō*, cannot function. I finish and say, "Please excuse me from the table." That's how we did it back home. Bill and Johnny jus' look at me. Then Johnny say, "Yeah, okay." Pili and I get up and head for the door. As we pass the other tables, people look at me and give me some sign, maybe shake of the head, a nod, a hello. All nice, trying to welcome me. It was to make me feel comfortable, but I was not used to having attention focused on me. One good thing, I didn't have to wash dishes. Jus' leave everything on the table after you eat.

I liked the dining room. It was clean and had curtains at the window. One time Beka told me follow her into the kitchen to thank Ma for the meal. Ma was Abigail Wilson, the manager of McVeigh Home. Pops Wilson was maintenance supervisor and they lived next to us. Beka nudge me.

"Thank you for breakfast."

"You want more?"

"No, no."

"Well, I hope you enjoy your stay with us and if there's anything you need don't hesitate to ask, okay?" Like this was one hotel.

There were lots of nice people. At the Bishop Home for the girls the Mother Superior was Sister Teresa, who was called Minnie Mouse behind her back because she was so short and tiny. At Baldwin Home for boys Brother Tarcissus was Da Man. Some guys they come in from the beach in shorts, any kine clothes, sweaty, dirty. Sometimes I would go eat at Baldwin Home with my friends and Brother Tarcissus would make the boys wash their hands, tell them to change clothes. But the boys not always listen, make joke with him. Everybody liked Brother Tarcissus but they pushed him to his limit. But even though they teased him, they gave him respect.

Anyway, that first night after dinner Pili and I went to the pool hall. Pili showed me how to crack the balls. Then some older guys start filtering out of the dining room. Some sat on the grass, talk story. Some watching Pili and me play. Johnny came over and asked if he could join us. Then some other guys joined us. I was new so I didn't catch the hint. Pili and I should have given up our cue sticks and let the older guys play. I jus' did whatever Pili did and he kept playing, so I did too. Finally I was embarrassed at playing so bad so we went home to the cottage.

I neva' see Beka for one year, neva' see Pili for three years, so I was trying to get to know them again, yeah? That night was hard to sleep 'cause Pili kept trying to clear his nose. I thought, "Jus' get toilet paper and blow real hard and all that stuff going fly out." But I didn't realize his nose had no more bridge so hard fo' blow. He jus' sniff, sniff, spray, wipe up with a towel. I was uncomfortable. What I didn't realize was that the bridge on Pili's nose was collapsed so he was jus' doing the best he could. Years later, the same thing happened to me.

We talked well into the late of night, he telling me things he wanted to share of the different people I would meet. I talked about the family at home: Daddy, Uncle Moku, Mama and Georgie, and Olga and Tweetie.

Did I tell you about Pili's radio? He had this radio that was between our beds. There was a trick to playing the radio. After maybe five, ten minutes, it would start to hum and you couldn't hear anything else. So Pili, with his hand swollen, would make a fist and wham! He hit the radio and I was so startled. "Dis damn radio," he would say. "That's how you gotta make 'em play every time." Another ten minutes the same thing. Finally I say, "Pili, turn 'em off already. The radio keep make da kine noise, you bang 'em, you bang 'em, make me nervous." But he ignored me.

In the morning the alarm sounded from the dining room, which we could hear all the way in our cottage. It was still dark outside. I dress quick, catch up to Pili. People coming from all directions for breakfast. Pili and I sit down. We are offered fried eggs, cereal, and coffee, tea or chocolate. Pili is tapping his plate for more but me, I thought the eggs was too raw. I like 'em well done. Beka is serving and she tells the waitresses, "My brothers are Mormons, so give 'em chocolate." Johnny comes over and says, "When Beka *pau* work we go for a drive, maybe Kalawao side." Bill was with us too and little by little I was able to notice the sounds happening in his throat. I was learning how to listen. I jus' tried not to stare. Hard, 'cause little puffs of air would come out when he spoke and the handkerchief would flutter. Then he whispers, "I'll see you two later."

Then Beka was at our table and lowered her voice.

"I have something to say to you two boys. Yesterday when you was playing pool and the older guys came and wanted to play they couldn't because you two was there. They didn't want to tell you folks to stop, but you two were in the way."

"Whenever this happens I want you to give up, so the older guys can play."

"But they was playing with us, too," I said.

"We was ova' there first," said Pili. "We playing and then they came."

"Neva' mind that," says Beka. "I don't want you boys in their way if something like that happens again. You hear me, Makia?"

"Yes."

"But we was there first." Pili, he no give up.

"No argue. I'm just telling you. You hear me, Pili?"

"Yeah." I recognize that quiver in his voice and I know he wants to cry.

"Johnny told me that some guys were complaining because they wanted to gamble, so please, Pili, don't cry. I jus' don't want anybody complain about our family, yeah? You, the baby, you the one. Sometimes you sassy to them and then I hear about it from Johnny."

"Den Johnny the one complained?" Pili shoots back.

"No, but he the one who told me about it. The guys wouldn't tell me so if it wasn't for Johnny I wouldn't hear any of this."

She turns to me and I can see the pain on her face.

"Mama not here with us to take care of you boys so we have to do the best we can and I need your help. So Makia, Pili, go back to the house, clean your room, sweep and mop. Afterward we go *holoholo* with Johnny, okay?

"We have one picnic."

I learning.

So Pili and me, we go back and clean the room. I can handle the sweeping and mopping but I had neva' fixed a bed before that came with a top sheet and a spread. They had the end tucked under the bed, which was a complete mystery to me.

So later the sounds of Johnny's Model A Ford jalopy up to the house.

"Howzit? You guys ready?" asks Johnny.

"You get any old clothes you can change into?" Beka asks me.

"This is old clothes."

"But that's a nice shirt. You go school with those clothes Monday. Fo' now, you get T-shirt?"

Now I'm thinking, "School? I thought this was a hospital." I'm thinking a little differently about this place. Pili gives me one of his T-shirts. It had a few small holes. I wasn't sure I wanted to use this shirt but then I thought, "What the hell."

Pili and I jump on the jalopy. Both of us sat in the back where we could hang our feet down above the road. Johnny gets the basket of food that Beka prepared the night before. Then she and Johnny got up in front. I never sat in a car like this before. The entire body from the dashboard to the back was removed. A lumber bench-like seat replaced the regular ones. The back part resembled a pickup truck and that is where we sat, our feet inches from the road. Beka show us the area of the McVeigh Home, the boys' home where Pali and Teddy and Stanley stay.

"I don't know those guys," I say.

"Those the guys went play pool with us yesterday," says Pili.

"Oh, dem." I turn to Johnny.

"Can I ask you something?"

"Yeah, okay."

"Dem guys were mad when we was playing pool?"

"No. Why you ask?" He sounded surprised.

"Dem guys was picking on you about us?" I ask.

"Nah! Dem guys every time tease me. They like me lose my head. I like tease 'em too when I get the chance. Best time to rattle 'em is jus' before they shoot." He's laughing.

By this time I am really liking Johnny. He didn't put me off when I asked him questions. "Gee," I thought, "Beka really lucky. She get one nice boyfriend. Not like Boy." Johnny neva' made me feel like one small kid. I thought he was kinda good looking, but I not sure. I not one girl so I no can tell. He look like one typical Portugee. The way his forehead came forward, his eyes looked like they were set deep. His mustache made him look real sharp. Like Errol Flynn, very dashing and smashing.

Then there's this big house, Mr. Judd's house. Johnny slows down, turns the car in the gates. Beka got out of the car, approached the gate, and pressed the buzzer.

"Who's there?"

"It's me, Pearl. I want to introduce my brother Elroy to you and Mr. Judd."

"Oh, that's so nice of you."

A *haole* lady appeared out of the house and she was very pretty. She turns her beautiful smile on me.

"My name is Eva Marie Judd and Lawrence is right inside. I'll call him. You wait a minute." She goes in the house. Since we weren't allowed to mingle, we had to wait outside. She comes back with a tall, fat *haole*. He looked kinda mean, man! But he was hospitable. His voice kinda low. Typical *haole*-type voice.

"It must be nice to see your sister and brothers again. Did you sleep well last night?"

"Okay."

"Homesick?"

"No."

"Well, your parents aren't here but at least you have Pearl and Bill to look after you and Earl." He finish that off with a big, toothy grin.

We climb back in the jalopy and wave goodbye. Beka shows me the nurses' quarters, the whole area called Staff Row. There's the American Legion cottage, the social hall with coconut trees around. We ended up at Baldwin Home to pick up Heed, who'd been on the plane with me. His Hawaiian name was Palili.

Heed and his older brother Johnny Silva was almost like family. In Papakōlea, Johnny had been having problems with his Mama, so Daddy and Mama took him in. After a while Mama says, "Johnny, you should go home, see your Mama." Johnny says, "I no like. You my Mama now." They made him go home anyway. He and Heed were always around. In fact, I always had a suspicion Heed got the disease by hanging around us.

"Palili," Beka turns to him, "I hope you like living at Baldwin Home. You know, when I first heard they were sending you Kalaupapa I went see Mr. Judd to see if there was some way you come McVeigh Home and live with us, but we don't have any more room. Jus' know we're here. No shy. If you like get away some night from Baldwin Home, you can come up and sleep."

We're going along the uneven, eroded path, turn around the corner to the right, when suddenly one truck comes into view. Beka screams and Johnny skids to a stop that had Pili and me rolling on our backs.

"Eh! Look where you going, eh!" Johnny yells, but he's laughing.

"*You* look where you driving. You McVeigh Home guys! Take it easy when you drive around Baldwin Home. Where you get your license, Sears and Roebuck?"

That was Kenzo Seki. He laughed and drove past us.

Johnny lurches to the left and we begin climbing up a slope. Steeper and steeper. That Model A of Johnny's sure had a lotta guts. We bounce and jostle side to side when suddenly Johnny gives a cowboy yell.

"Yeehaw! Heed, Makia, what you think of this ride? Good, eh? Good for the lumbago, this kine ride. Shake 'em up real good!"

As we pop the rise we drop in this little rut. Our 'ōkoles lift up and slam back down. Ow! I look at Pili. He's clinging to the back of the front seat trying to keep his 'ōkole from bouncing off the wood floor.

We go down a slope and stop beside a stone wall.

"This the Protestant church. You can go in and look if you like," Beka says.

"No, I don't think so. Look too spooky." Johnny laughs and we drive on till we come to the Damien church. Beka says come and we go inside. The smell of age came through the door. The wood was so worn, like time removed all the paint. To the left was an old organ with many broken keys. It was so quiet you could hear our footsteps.

"This is Father Damien's church," said Beka. "The Catholics don't hold services here anymore but they hire somebody to clean the yard." I neva' been in a Catholic church before because I was Mormon. I had this sense of wrong, being in this church that mine was opposed to.

"Beka, get ghosts over hea?" I asked.

"Wassamatta you, Makia? This one church! You look some more and when you folks *pau*, get on the car." And she walks out.

"Hey Pili, I can play organ?"

"Da thing stay broke, but you can go try." But before I can make a move he walks in front of me and sits on the stool. His feet on the pedals and he's pumping but no sound. Nothing. Then he let me try. My fingers ran along the keyboard. I wished I could play the organ. A dumb wish at the moment. I thought I better leave before the Catholic spirits try pull me back. My skin began to crawl. I ran for the car. Beka sees me, her eyes wide with alarm.

"Wassamatta?"

"Oh Beka, inside spooky! I think get ghosts inside."

"No be silly. That's all in your mind."

Jus' then a loud scream comes from the church and Heed comes flying outta there, rushing to the car, his eyes big like mine. Now Beka truly alarmed.

"Wassamatta, Palili?"

"Your goddamn bruddah! Your goddamn kid bruddah! He went scream and came running toward me. I take off!" Then Pili is in the doorway laughing and laughing.

Beka tried apologizing to Heed but he closed in on himself. He stayed aloof from us the rest of the afternoon. As we drove away I tried to figure out why I was so scared. "'Cause Catholic, that's why," I thought.

We went to the Federal, used to be the Federal Hospital. Pili has a hard time breathing and he blow his nose and get blood.

"You see what happens," scolds Beka."You running around like that and now you get reaction. When you get back Dr. Sloan going yell at me."

I could see the frustration on Pili's face and I felt shitty making him run around with me. I was scared to think of how sick he really was. I could feel my tears, watching Pili slump over, sobbing, struggling to breathe. Then Beka give in to her tears.

"Stop crying, Pili. You have to take care. Otherwise docta' no let you come out for Makia's birthday next week. Stop crying." She pull us together and we huddle.

Later on Johnny pulls the car to a stop. "You see that spot way down there? That's where we call Nehoa. Some guys call 'em The Flat. You see the two small islands down there on this side? You continue on to shore and you see that ridge. Well, that ends Kalaupapa on this side. So between Nehoa and Wailolu Point, this all Kalaupapa. This a pretty big place. We can go all this place. Anytime we like."

My eyes were feasting on all these new sights and my heart jus' overflowing with aloha for this place. If I had to be sent anywhere, I couldn't have been sent to a better place. ✦

MALIHINI—NEWCOMER

Days followed days like a long hot summer
From sunrise to sunset, each holding perfect moments.
For it was a long ago time, when, as a child I yearned for dreams
that would never happen.
In the dark of night, I yearn for a tender voice to soothe the
fears, and reach for arms to comfort me,
But there were none to help chase the threatening shadows
away.

An aborted gasp of alarm could not stifle the flow of tears.
Though the piercing heartache distresses, and awakens me,
As a cry of "Mama" escapes my lips,
Dissipating to nothingness,
Unheard by anyone else, but me.
Even afterward, I was not sure if I cried,
Nor if I heard anything at all.

Even now, I can still feel the anguish of separation,
I can still feel Mama's agony as she hugged me,
And said, "Why me, Lord!"
While her tears streamed down from her face, and onto mine,
As she kissed me goodbye.
The lingering taste of her tears haunting me for days afterward.

It was not then that I felt the ache,
It was a month, a whole month before I recalled that moment,
Then came the pain, and again the tears.
I faced each morning with a bright smile, and a warm hello,
For the tears and sorrow were only for the nights.

I shared each day with Pili, Beka and Pu'a,
And the days were filled with new experiences, new faces.
Some of them were nice, clean, friendly faces,

Unmarked by the dread;
Then there were others … and others still …
Whose heartrending tragedies were all too painfully obvious.
And yet, in spite of their struggles,
They always had a kind word for the newcomer.

Sadly, though, there were many for whom the bells tolled;
For they gave up the struggle.
We all had a role in this drama,
Playing out our parts toward an end that no one acknowledged,
But, of course, all were aware of.

The days passed into weeks, into months, into years.
Newcomers came after me; some younger, some older.
Each passing of time marked the loss of yearning for home,
To be replaced by despair, then indifference, then acceptance …
Until finally, "I'll never leave this place,
And be damned glad of it!"

Chapter Three

I started having a change in the way I saw this place. I thought sick people had high fevers and stayed in bed, incapacitated-like. These people didn't walk around in pajamas and bathrobes. Everybody smiled. Except for the few marks on the face and on the hands, they didn't look sick. But of course they were. We all were.

Kalaupapa started to be like a playground for me. School only for three hours in the morning, seven-thirty to ten-thirty. All I cared was I didn't have to work taro patch anymore. On Oʻahu every weekend my parents made us work in the taro patch out in Lāʻie. The whole family pitched in because this was our food source in times there wasn't anything else, like during the war. The work was hard and the water so cold. Pili and I made a game of it but even so it was tough, so I was glad I didn't have to work anymore. As far as I was concerned, Kalaupapa was paradise.

The school was small and I didn't think it was a proper school. We were of all different ages in the same classroom, twelve boys and three girls. Our teacher was a patient herself. I don't know if she was a trained teacher or what. What did I learn?

Nothing, really. They gave me *The Pilgrim's Progress*, which I had already read at Pauoa Elementary. I was so mad. Why is she giving this book to me? I figured out that the books we had were old and discarded. They were the ones the public schools on Oʻahu were no longer using. We never got any new books, the ones regular students were using on Oʻahu. How would that make you feel? I was so mad. You know me, I started running off at the mouth. I wouldn't let the matter die. The teacher was sick of me complaining and threatened to kick me out of school. I was scared Mama would find out so I decided it would be better if I just shut up.

I wasn't what you would call a good student but something caught my attention. Poetry. I would look at how the words lay in the sentence. I would notice how sometimes there was more than one meaning. I asked myself, "How can they write stuff like this?" It was almost like music, this poetry. It had rhythm. It sounded good when you read it aloud. You could even sing to it if you wanted to.

I remember one time at Pauoa Elementary, there were six of us students given poems to read to the whole school at assembly. This was a very big thing and considered an honor, so of course we had to dress up. I wore a nice shirt and I made sure to wear shoes that day. The other students took their turns and went on the stage to recite their poems, which they had all memorized. I was standing there, waiting, when suddenly I thought, "Oh geez, no, something is wrong. I shouldn't be dressed like this." I tore off my shirt and kicked off my socks and shoes. I rolled up my pant legs. And that's how I walked on stage. My poem was "The Song of Hiawatha," by Henry Wadsworth Longfellow.

> By the shore of Gitche Gumee,
> By the shining Big-Sea-Water,
> At the doorway of his wigwam,
> In the pleasant Summer morning,
> Hiawatha stood and waited.
> All the air was full of freshness,
> All the earth was bright and joyous,
> And before him, through the sunshine,
> Westward toward the neighboring forest
> Passed in golden swarms the Ahmo,
> Passed the bees, the honey-makers,
> Burning, singing in the sunshine.

How I loved that poem. For Hiawatha, I changed my clothes.

To honor him.

I never thought about writing poems of my own. I didn't think I was smart enough. Back then no one told me I was smart enough. It was not the way of my parents to encourage us to do anything except work taro patch. Sometimes us kids would make up songs … "P.A., P.A., K.O., L.E.A., that stands for Papakōlea." Stuff like that.

In school I didn't want anybody to know I was getting hooked on books. I kept it to myself, otherwise they call me *māhū*. I didn't want them to know how much I loved learning. So you can see why I got so mad having to read these old books. After awhile you get the feeling Kalaupapa is not really connected to the real world.

Beka made me go to church, the Mormon church, because Daddy was originally from Lā'ie, where there are a lot of Mormons, so we knew this church. Only here they didn't tell us we were sinners.

We had movies twice a week, Mondays and Fridays. There was only one land access to the settlement, the switchback mule trail along the cliff. Someone would go up the trail with our mail, then come down with new mail and a movie reel. So we would see movies on those nights. Jus' like back home, Beka was like my Mama, giving me lickin's when I was bad. At home, Mama would whack us with a stick. Bend us over on her lap and take a stick and give it to us on the *'ōkole*. Man, it hurt. Here, one of my punishments was not being allowed to go to the movies. I had to stay in my room. Yeah, my sistah could be mean.

THE GOLDEN WALL THEATER

In the old days Daddy used to give Pili and me a quarter each to go Golden Wall Theater on School Street. Our favorite theater, that. Da kine real bedbug theater. And every Sunday after church with our twenty-five cents in our pockets we'd walk all the way down Pauoa Road until we came to Fort Street, which in those days intersected

Pauoa. Then we walk down Fort Street to School. Nine cents out of our twenty-five would get each of us into the movie. One penny, bubble gum, ten cents for one plate spaghetti or macaroni salad, five cents for shaved ice … with two flavors! That was our Sunday treat.

On this particular Sunday, for whatever reason, I forget why, we decided to go to Roosevelt Theater, which was a step higher in class than Golden Wall. I don't know why, but we came out of the theater completely broke. We didn't have any money to get something to eat, so Pili came up with a great idea.

"Eh 'Kia. We go ask Auntie Lei for money."

"Who dat, Auntie Lei? We no more Auntie Lei."

"We get. We get. I went meet her with Beka. She stay over here."

"Okay, I follow you."

We turn down an alley, then take a right along an open court of closed doors. In the far corner we climb a long set of steps, then on the second landing, two doors to the right. Pili stop and turn to me. He look like he's losing some of his nerve.

"You like knock?" he asks.

"No. That's your Auntie. I don't know her."

So Pili knock. And knock. And knock. The sound echoes. I take a step back in case I need to escape. Still he knocking. By this time I'm way back by the stairs watching him. Then I hear.

"Yes? Who is that?"

"Auntie Lei, is me, Pilipili."

"Who?"

"Pilipili."

"Oh. Just a minute. I be there."

She open the door partway. She didn't see me.

"Come inside, Pili. How are you?"

"I fine, Auntie Lei. I can have money?"

"What?"

Pili walked in and she closed the door. I was left standing outside. I could hear their voices coming through the transom. A few minutes later Pili comes out holding a dollar.

"Where is your brother?" she asks. She turns and looks right at me. She holds out another dollar for me and I am embarrassed. I sensed this was wrong. We weren't allowed to ask strangers for money. We weren't allowed to ask anyone for money. But Pili insisted this was okay because she was our Auntie. A feeling of shame held me in place.

"This is for you," she said again. The buzzers were going off in my mind and I wanted to refuse it but I was torn because I really did want to take it.

"Here, take it. I have to go back to sleep."

"Sorry we spoiled your sleep," I said.

"That's okay." Then she closed the door.

I couldn't believe it. A whole dollar for Pili? A whole one for me? And from an Auntie I neva' met before. And then Pili has another bright idea. We go circus. I couldn't believe this bruddah of mine. He had gone completely beyond right or wrong on how we got this money and now was bent on spending it. Again though, like a *lōlō*, I said okay. So Pili walks, with me tagging along, to Beretania until we get to 'A'ala Park, where there are tents and stuff. He head straight for the pony rides.

Soon all the children on ponies are being led around in a circle. Mine starts to kick. And kick. And kick. Each time my *'ōkole* would lift a few inches off the saddle and I was scared as hell. I glance at Pili and he's encouraging his pony to go faster.

Pili took a few more rides and I went over to check out this magician. When I went looking for Pili again he was at the food stand stuffing himself with hot dogs, soda, ice cream and cotton candy. I bought a hot dog and soda and decided not to spend any more, thinking I could save it for later.

"Eh Pili, I think we betta go home now."

"What time now?"

"About four-thirty."

"I like ride Ferris wheel and then we go home, okay?"

"Late already, we betta go home."

"Come on, 'Kia. Only one ride. Then we go."

He turn his back on me and scoots off to the Ferris wheel. I couldn't leave him here alone. I get it from Mama. Oh shit, I might as well go, too.

On our way home Pili was happy as a mynah bird after a fabulous day going to movies, bumming money from that lady, pony rides, Ferris wheel, and food. Yeah. He had a good day. Me, on the other hand, I had some misgivings.

A few days later Mama called the two of us. She and Beka were in the kitchen. The looks on their faces said we were in trouble.

"Makia, how come you went to that lady, ask for money? Who said you folks can go around like bums and beg for money?"

"What lady? What money?" I'm thinking. Then it dawns on me.

"Pili said she was our Auntie so was okay to ask for money."

We both got lickin's. ❧

Chapter Four

I started noticing girls about then, but I was too shy to do anything about it. Anyway there weren't that many of them around. One time my brother was talking to two girls through the window of the hospital. I never saw them before. I thought, "They're young, our age, how come they not in school?" Turns out they had tuberculosis.

I got my first job at Kalaupapa, paying twenty-five cents an hour. Oh boy, twenty-five cents an hour was a big thing to me. I had to water these potted plants, mostly poinsettia. At Christmas, these plants were sent to all the homes, churches, and whatever. After Christmas, they came back and I would take care of them again. It was a lot easier than working taro patch and I was making money, too. Not that there was anything to buy.

I made friends with some other boys, Henry Nalaielua, Danny Hashimoto, Eddie Marks, Frankie Leong, who we called Donkey (I came over on the plane with his brother), and Bernard Punikai'a. After school Pili and I would go home for lunch and then the afternoon we had to ourselves. Us boys always went swimming down by the pier. All I wanted to do is swim, fish, go up into the mountains. That was the life. No matter how sick I was, the night before I would make sure I would be in top shape to go up the mountains.

Pili took me all these different places to go swimming. You know the Mormon church? The road goes past and cuts down by the beach side and takes a turn by the carpenter shops. Behind there was a stone crusher, this big thing that would demolish the rocks they gathered near the river. They used that stuff to repair the roads. We went swimming near there. Lots of fish. I was always afraid of the eels. Anywhere you got rocky areas, there's going to be eels. Yellowish with black spots, what's the name of that eel? I can't remember now. I never got bit but I've seen it bite fish. Swoop! Just like that.

Nobody bother us swimming 'cause good for the wounds, yeah? Saltwater good for the sores, clean 'em out, you know, all the *pilau*, the filth, but too much no good. The old-timers, they say the saltwater and the sunshine good for Vitamin D, but don't go every day or you going get ulcers. So sometimes we swim, sometimes we climb the rocks, pick *'opihi*, eat 'em right there.

Sometimes the girls would come down, crack jokes with us. But I was too shy to, you know, get in a conversation. One time some nurses came down to swim. Oh, that changed everything. Patients and *kōkuas* neva' mix, yeah? These were *haole* nurses from outside. Their skin so white and clean, no bumps, no ulcers. We didn't go in the water. Nobody said anything, but we knew not to. We just sit and watch.

And then one of the nurses dive off the wall. Beautiful dive. When she surfaced her breasts were totally exposed 'cause her swimsuit fell down. Our eyes pop! I never saw any like that before. Her body was so white. But no big thing to her. She just pull up the straps of the swimsuit and got out of the water. Her name was Lee. I really liked her and I was a little jealous of Pili because this nurse liked him and sometimes she talked about adopting him. I don't know if she was kidding but I was jealous 'cause Pili get her attention.

The thing about the *kōkuas* and the other people from topside, you can see the attitude is all different. They go wherever they like, no need ask permission. They just comfortable walking around, doing whatever, no shame. For years I would hide my hands whenever I was around outsiders.

You know, in the old days, before Kalaupapa was a leprosy settlement, normal Hawaiians used to live here. They were taro farmers and fishermen. But when the government took over they had to leave. A few of them ran up into the valleys because they didn't want to leave their land, but today, it's only patients. Some of the first patients tried to take over the farms, but you know, they didn't have the strength to pull taro. If there wasn't enough food they would have to scavenge. If you know the *ʻāina*, the land, you can eat, you can survive. You know which plants to eat and how to use the others to make things like bowls and medicine. And everybody fished. This area had the best fishing and still does if you know where to go.

Mountain apple was my favorite food. We used to play lumberjack. Mountain apple jack. They were big trees so we would cut the trees down and gather all the apples and eat most of them before we got home. Terrible, yeah? *Lilikoʻi,* too.

One day I saw a pool off the trail. When we went into the valley we went through the right and came out the other side. You make the turn and you see water slowly flowing out of the porous rock. Wow. The whole wall, glassy with water. I put my mouth to it and filled up with water. Fabulous. The water was coming out the mountain. So fabulous. So cold. When there's a lot of rain topside, the river flows. When you go into the valleys you can see one side higher. Nobody could be living there, it was too narrow, but then behind might be big and open. I had a dream of disappearing up into one of those valleys, nobody find me. That's as far as it went. A dream.

Bernard Punikaiʻa and I would go up in the valleys and sometimes there would be this old shed where someone used to live in the old days, maybe one of the original farmers hiding out from the government. Sometimes we would go to the Damien church, which I learned was called St. Philomena's. Bernard showed me the holes in the floor of the church. When Damien was the priest there he punched holes in the floor and made one ti leaf like a funnel so the patients would have somewhere to spit when they had to clear their phlegm.

I thought this guy Damien was crazy. Come all the way to Hawaiʻi from Belgium only to catch a disease and die. What was he thinking? But the more I learned about him the more I respected that man. There were priests before but none of them stayed and lived with the patients. None of them bothered to learn the Hawaiian language and our culture. The Protestants and Mormons didn't talk about him much because he was a Catholic, but I knew how I felt. He was one of us.

When he died he wanted to be buried in Kalaupapa but the king of Belgium had him dug up and sent back to Belgium. I heard stories about how the patients wailed, *"Auwē!"* when they carried his casket away. That's why it was so important for me to go to Belgium years later and touch his casket in his tomb.

DAMIEN'S CHURCH

In the night sky, the moon rises full, its luminescence bathing the
        ground in ghostly silver.
Damien's church is awash in an eerie spectrelike glow, its dark windows
        like empty sockets peering out across a field.
Through some ironwood pine, moonbeams flicker in and out; but in
        the denser, more prominent surrounding trees, all beneath
        is cloaked in absolute black, where the dank smell of decay,
        molding vegetation prevail.
There is no wind, as if moonlight has chased the breeze away.
The air is still, an aura breathing softly.

Stone walls that stand on both sides of the road in front of the church,
        lie partially hidden in the trees' gloom.
Faint shadowy outlines of rock and pothole pockmark the path;
Silhouettes of scraggily grasses cluster here and there,
        the faint odor of dust clinging close.
At the edge of the open field, fence posts stand patiently, in single file,
        to enclose the boundaries on the seaward side of the paddock.
Bulky shapes low on the ground are nameless graves from another
        time.
The surf below the cliffs whispers ceaselessly.
Light billowing clouds of salty air rise up from the shore below,

floating upward,
an ethereal bank just above and beyond the edge of the bluff.

In my mind, I hear the echo of voices;
I hear their songs, their laughter, their anger and their fears.
I hear their cries of pain, and their cries of sorrow that would shatter
any human heart.
I hear "Mama! Mama!"
and garbled voices in final communion.
I hear the tolling of the bell as one more passes on;
And a choir of voices raised in song, in celebration of the end of
suffering.
I hear all this, and I also hear silence, the profound silence of
resignation, of total surrender.

And I weep.
I weep for the passing of these my fellow sufferers;
But I am grateful.
I am humbled by the thought that their suffering without respite
has made my suffering less painful;
I am humbled, too, by the thought of their enduring the shame of exile,
which makes it easier to face the world.
Yet, I have fears, for there is no one out there to take up our cause
anymore.
Our champion is dead.
His hard work, his commitment has made him famous,
and he is loved the world over,
but he is dead, buried in the land
among those to whom he gave solace, comfort, and
companionship, succumbing finally to the dreaded scourge
himself.

Am I worthy enough to travel his path? In his footsteps?
To tread in his steps, on his path,
that lead to the grave beside the church he loved?

I bask in the moonglow these one hundred and seventy-five
years later under the towering cliffs of Kalawao,
enveloped by the presence of Kamiana,
The Torchbearer, whose flame still lights the way. ✦

Chapter Five

Spending time with my sister and two brothers I learned a lot about the family, stuff Mama and Daddy didn't talk about. I learned Mama had a baby before Bill. She was a teenager and she ran away and had a daughter named Angela with a guy in the family that took her in. That daughter stayed topside Molokaʻi with the father.

Beka and Johnny had a baby, too, before I came. Baby Abraham. He died really early and was buried in Lāʻie.

I also learned that it was my step-grandfather who brought the disease into the family. My real grandfather died and my grandmother remarried and that man she married was the first to get it. My grandmother *hānaied* my oldest brother Bill and he came to live with them. That's how he got it. Daddy's house in Papakōlea already had so many kids and sometimes Mama would take in kids in the neighborhood who were having problems, so, as the oldest, Bill went to help out our grandmother.

Bill said the last time he saw our step-grandfather he was walking down the street with a suitcase in one hand and a shoulder bag in the other. He was going to report to Kalihi Hospital, where we dropped off Pili. He died two years later. I don't know what I feel for this man. If our grandmother hadn't remarried, maybe we all would have escaped the disease. I know he didn't mean to bring leprosy into the family. I was too young to know him, but Bill said he loved my grandmother.

I was always close to Pili and I thought maybe I could get to know Bill, but he was kind of distant. I think he had some resentment toward us because we were raised with my parents and he was not. And, of course, it was at my grandmother's house where he got the disease, so yeah, some resentment.

I remember one time he was in front of the mirror in the bathroom. He was trying to clear his throat, trying to get the *hanabata* out. I was standing by the door and I saw that metal thing in his throat. He sees me in the mirror and says, "What the hell you looking at?"

One time he tried to talk to me but I had my back to him so I deaf to his clicks. So he swing this rope, whip me across the back. Not hurt, but it shocked me and from then on I had a different feeling about him. "Damn bugga," I thought. "Neva' have to hit me."

His relationship with Pili was much better, I suppose because Pili was there early on when he could still talk. Anyway, no matter what kine sounds Bill would make Pili understood what he was saying.

One week after I came Kalaupapa I started receiving sulfone drugs. Did nothing, really. My health was in decline and I have only myself to blame. I ruined my own health with the hunting and diving. I was so active as a youngster. I didn't take care of my feet. I had a lot of ulcers that I ignored. We went barefoot mostly and there was no feeling when we got a cut. The ulcers were so bad and lasted for years until they finally had to take off my toes, two of them on the right foot. I was fifteen. I had an ulcer at the base of the small toe. On the bone I had an ulcer and underneath the middle toe. I was too immature, too dumb to know. I would cover my wounds with a Band-Aid and go back up the mountain hunting. I did that over and over again. I didn't know you have to immobilize so the wound can heal. Takes a long time. The bacteria eats the meat and you don't feel it unless you're really badly infected. So we all had raw wounds and holes in our legs down to the bone.

It was common for the government to send some of us to Carville, Louisiana, for treatment if our medical problems were serious. There's a big leprosarium there where they treat patients from all over the United States. A few of us went and the doctors would look us over and do what they could. They tried to operate to open our crab hands, but it wasn't a big improvement.

Because patients tend to lose eyebrows, they even tried to graft hair from our scalps onto our foreheads. They did this one guy and I thought, "Oh, God, how awful." He looked like he had two black horseshoes on his face. They did my eyebrows, too, and it wasn't that bad, but the hair fell out eventually.

Back in Kalaupapa, the sulfone drugs helped a lot of patients, so, after awhile, the government allowed visitors. We would see them all dressed up, looking out of place. Eh, who dat? My parents came when they could, but none of the other relatives. They would stay in the visitors' quarters. There were the same precautions as at Kalihi Hospital, but more because Kalaupapa had the more serious patients. Whatever the visitors ate they had to bring with them from Oʻahu. We would sneak food to them, ʻopihi, stuff like that. It was good to see my parents but none of us liked to see them so sad.

I still went up into the mountains whenever I could. I didn't have a car so I would walk all the way from town to the first valley, Waihānau, which means "waters of birth." Eddie Marks had a rifle, which was illegal at the time. I think he got it from his brother Richard, who was later made sheriff. Eddie was the one who really got me into hunting. There was Eddie, me, Jubilee, I can't remember all their names.

It seemed the whole land was set aside for us. We'd go up this valley and separate, one group up one side, the others up the other side. We had an agreement that we never shot down the valley in case the other guys are coming that way. Always shoot up the mountainside. One group hears shooting, we know, oh, they found something. We run up the hill. Always a lot of goats, sometimes pig, and cattle, though we never shot the cattle. They make you run, the cattle, especially the bull.

The Filipinos, they love to eat goat, so they would take it home and cook it. If I had goat I just brought it home for the dog. I didn't eat goat. Until I gave some to my friend Domias. Nice guy with claw hands. He cooked the goat and invited me over to eat. That was the first time. It was okay. Domias said, "It's different if you catch them live and slaughter them later, because you can cook them with the blood." When I heard that I thought, "What the hell?" We did that, too, with pig. The first thing Daddy would do is rap the pig on the head and clean the throat and Mama would get one pot to catch the blood. You clean up the pig, take off the hair and open it up and clean the inside. Daddy used to work for the Navy at the ʻAiea Naval Hospital, then later Barbers Point, so he would make a party whenever we had pig. The guys would come up after work to eat and gamble. We put the benches in the driveway, covered with paper, we get the sodas, the beer. We'd make a whole day of it. The first thing, after killing the pig, we eat the intestines, the tripe. That's our breakfast, the best.

Then us kids would tend to the *imu*, the fire pit. Put the pig in the ground, cover with chicken wire and burlap, then the dirt. Anytime you see the steam come up through the dirt, you gotta cover 'em. What memories.

One time in Kalaupapa we decided to catch goats to raise. You go up, there's this shelf on the mountain. All this debris from topside would come down after a rain, dirt, trees, stuff like that. It would pile up on top the boulders and make this slope. On top was like a cushion. So there we were when Eddie's dogs had cornered these goats, eight billies, a nanny and two babies. The first thing Eddie did was get a rope and tie the nanny to a tree. But he forgot his knife so he asked me to go down the hill and get a sharp rock and we bang, bang on the rope until it cuts. But all of a sudden the billies started jumping off the soft slope. Then the nanny jumped but she got snagged by the rope. So we bang, bang on the rope. Finally the nanny fell. She was going to get away but the dogs were there. Eddie took the mother and put her in a pigsty to raise. I took home one of the baby goats. Stuff like that.

We used to go shooting dove, too. The big dove. There's more to eat in those doves than the smaller ones. You pull the feathers, clean the stomach, chop off the head, the feet. The skin is the best part, especially if you fry it up. Maybe two doves a person. One not enough.

I was used to hunting birds because we used to go after grey dove in Papakōlea. We would shoot them with slingshots that we made from inner tubes. In Kalaupapa sometimes you were lucky to get pheasant. And deer, if you had a big gun, at least a 30-30, Army carbine. I had one of those. I had four guns, all illegal. My brother David had gone into the service. When he came out and asked what I wanted I said, "A rifle." He said, "I can get." A .22 rifle, slide action. My brother Bill had a camera and he liked to take pictures. He had one of those tripod stands, which he put in a box. So when David came to visit they put the rifle in the box so no one could see it. I don't know where all my guns are now. I gave them all away.

We loved to go up into the mountains because that was freedom to us. No one to ask where we going, what we doing. No one to shame us. Back in the settlement, we were prisoners. Our lives were so structured, all the time somebody on our backs, so when we were off together, us boys, we kind of went wild. And the valleys and mountains of Kalaupapa were the best place to do that. Oh, the fun we had. That's what I remember about that terrible time. That's what I choose to remember. Us boys laughing and playing, going up into the hills. At our age normal kids start thinking about what they want to do, what they want to be. Not us. We didn't think about the future and no one encouraged us to think about the future.

GROWING UP AT PAPAKŌLEA

My family had a taro patch, you know where the Polynesian Cultural Center is? That used to be all taro land before, and so every Saturday, oh, hard work, let me tell you. Early in the morning we had to get up to leave the house at least by seven o'clock.

So my kid brother and I sleep in the same bed, old-style double. The middle sink down, so if you sleep on the side, you roll down the center. So every time we try fo' be the one in the center 'cause the other guy going have hard time. If get more than two people in the bed, the one who stay in the middle going get all the blanket because the one on the end when he pull, the other guy on the end no more blanket, so quite often we fighting in the bed. And me, I sleep next to my brother Pili, he's the baby. So I sleep close to him to keep warm.

Early in the morning Mama get hustling everybody up. I hear Mama making noise. I hit Pili. I say, "Mama coming, get up." He says, "Yeah, yeah, you too, wake up." And Mama says, "If you guys don't get up you going get lickin's." Oh man, we get up.

Breakfast was hurry-up job. Maybe cracker, chocolate, Vienna sausage, whatever. Leftovers usually. Seven o'clock we in the old station wagon, crossing Papakōlea bridge, then we heading up toward Nu'uanu Pali. Mama and Daddy in front, Pilipili, the baby, stay up front maybe on Mama's lap. Me and my brother George in the center, cheat seat, and my Uncle Moku get the last seat in the station wagon. You know, cold, yeah, in the morning, so kinda curl up and sleep. And that's when my uncle decide to smoke and you know the car come stink with all that smell. So I gotta open up the window and they get hard time sleep because so cold.

Now my brother and I have this game we play. I look my side-and oh, plenty stuff, so I yell to Pili, I say, "Pili, the side of the car you stay is your side. This side my side." So I look and I say, "Look, my side get tree, get one house, get road, oh, I get cow! Your side no more nothing. You get junk side. I get horse, and look, I get one stream, all kind stuff." And I name everything on my side. And because I was older I had better control of the language than Pili, I can outtalk him.

The next thing I hear Mama, "Baby, look, you get big store, one church, you get park." Me, I'm thinking, "Eh, that's not fair 'cause Mama helping out Pili." So I say, "Eh, I get *kalakoa* cow, I get one, two, I get three horse." I name everything.

Next thing I know I hear Uncle Moku say, "Baby, look this side, get two motorcycle, get park over there." And I think, "How come, now Uncle Moku helping out? Man, that's not fair." And I try to think of the worst thing to do just to get back at them.

Oh, oh, and I remember just past Kāne'ohe, just before He'eia State Park, there's this long bridge, used to say it was the longest bridge in the Islands. Us kids we call it the Stink Fart Bridge because the swamp inside, the smell used to come across the bridge, was so stink. And what we tried to do is hold our breath until we get across the bridge.

So just as we go to hit the bridge I yell out, "Pilipili, this Stink Fart Bridge for you, Mama, and Uncle Moku." And then I close my nose, I shut my eye and curl up and I wait until I can start breathing again. And then when I open my nose, *auwē!* I hear my Mama say, "Makia, you going get lickin'!"

The next thing I hear Daddy going after Mama, "Eh *nei*, you know the boys like that, honey, they playing the game." Mama and Daddy start fighting.

We go down the road and oh, Mama and Daddy still fighting. I tell Pili, "Eh, Pili, look, I get one big house my side." And Daddy tell me, "'Nough, Makia! 'Nough already, bum by you boys only fight." And then we reach the taro patch about an hour later and let me tell you that water is cold 'cause the cold air is coming down *mauka* side, I no like jump in the water. Now, we had waterland taro, which meant we had to have a lot of water inside. So we get there and we prolonging the time before getting into the water. Well, Mama always on our case, make sure we stay coming along with the rest of the family. The older ones they usually pull taro. When we were babies they used to try to make work look like fun. So while Mama and Daddy pulling the taro, me and Pili stay playing in the *'auwai*, that's the irrigation ditch. So Mama say, "Makia, come, come, take this taro to Daddy." We were so small only one taro was enough for us to carry because our hands were clumsy, we couldn't hold more than one plant. So carry one taro, run to the *'auwai*, and everybody laugh and clap, eh, you have good fun because everybody cheering you on. Gee, you run back, get one more taro, and they clap again and laugh. Work was fun. And because we were babies we worked naked. As the years went by we begin to learn that work not fun. Because as you get older, you have no choice.

So from carrying the taro we graduated to weeding the taro patch. Now you get one whole taro patch and only me and Pili pulling weeds. And in the morning, no matter how fresh you are, gee, by nine o'clock, the sun is beating on your back and the taro plant so tall, leaves so big, kind of like umbrella. After a while we get tired. Ah geez, we lay in the mud. We pull the weeds, pull ourselves like one *'o'opu* in the water, go to the next bed.

Bum by we get more tired, aah, just pick up mud and pile 'em up on top the weeds. What happens because we out of sight, Mama always suspicious. She look around, she no see us. As I said, the taro plant so tall. Sometimes we hide deliberately from Mama so we no need work. We put our head on the dry bed of that taro and go sleep, but Mama was smart.

She pick up a big pile of mud and she throw it in the taro patch. Well, what happens is the mud just breaks apart, sprinkles against the leaves like a shotgun, splattering against the leaves. We jump up. "No, please, we no like lickin's!"

That was every week. And then when I was twelve years old we found out I had leprosy. To be honest with you I wasn't sad because I didn't have to work taro patch anymore. ❧

Chapter Six

Back in Damien's day, he started a band. Just patients with whatever donated instruments to play at special occasions, stuff like that. So the administrators at Kalaupapa always wanted to continue that. Pili and I joined Mr. Judd's Boys' Band, ha! We learned 'ukulele, guitar, bass, trumpet, though you had to still have good hands to play, yeah? Trombone was the easiest because it was slide action. Pili and I had alto horns. Bernard wasn't in the band because by that time his mouth was bad and he couldn't blow.

There was this kōkua worker who was a musician and he organized us. We didn't see him every day so we would just take the instruments home and practice. No real training. I wouldn't say we were good, but we weren't terrible. Just so-so. There were a bunch of us, I don't remember the names, but not all kids. Some were already in their twenties. We didn't really click the first time we played. It was hilarious. It was at one of these events the women organized for the men, kind of like Valentine's Day.

Mr. Judd, I don't know if you ever saw a picture of him, big *haole* guy, standing in the center. And we start to play, um pa pa, um pa pa, like that. Me and my brother were awful. I looking at Pili and he looking at me, like, "You not doing it right," "No, *you* not doing it right." Then Mr. Judd looking at us mouthing the word, "Blow!" So I blow real loud and, oh God, it was so flat. Then we start cracking up. Mr. Judd was really upset.

Every year there were new medications. Not everyone in the community got it. I was one of twelve patients to be given promizole. After that the drug promine. Didn't cure me. It was discouraging.

We would get tested once a month. I noticed my hands were getting more numb. When we played volleyball, I would hit the ball and my fingers would split and I couldn't feel it. By that time I had what you call crab hands. They looked like stumps and the fingernails were like claws. They had no feeling. Very dangerous. If I was cooking anything and I touched hot stuff, I didn't feel. I would get a blister and oh, shucks, it would get worse. Eventually my fingers ulcerated. This forefinger, the tip, had to be removed. This fourth finger still here, small fingers here, but cannot use. This was happening to everyone, yet we were still able to do a lot. Sometimes to carry things I would use my mouth.

My friends and I were never really concerned about the disease. We were still so young and didn't think about it. Didn't want to think about it. But every time we ran into the older patients, we saw our future. Many lived in the cottages on the far side of the settlement. We didn't see them often. When we had dances, movies, or entertainment, they never came. In my own family, Bill was now in a wheelchair. You could see the damage on his face, no eyebrows, scars here and there. Beka always looked okay but Pili, even from childhood, showed signs of the disease, though his hands were better than mine. That was good because he would need them years later to find work outside of Kalaupapa.

Since Pili wasn't a hunter, he did other things. He got to know a lot of the blind guys in the settlement. Sometimes I would go with him to visit. They were neat. We would sit and talk story. They always had good stories. This, too, was a glimpse of my future. I would remember them years later when I started to lose my own sight.

My sister was getting married to Johnny at this point so she and Bill made a deal. Each one would take one of us. Turns out we both wanted to go live with my sister because we didn't want to stay with Bill.

Most of the time, though, we stayed with Tony and Jimmy. Anthony and James Davidson were *haole*. Their skin was white. There weren't too many *haoles* at Kalaupapa, so you remembered them. Blondie, the little girl at Kalihi Hospital, was eventually sent here. She looked *haole* but she was Portugee.

I met the Davidsons through Donkey. One day after we went hunting Donkey took me to this house. We looked in the window. Nobody around. I see him shaking the window. I'm not too sure about this. Next thing I see Donkey's unlocking the door. We walk inside, look around, nobody. Donkey goes straight to the kitchen. He cooks up these doves we just shot. Made pancakes, too. I go to the parlor and listen to the radio while Donkey is cooking. Finally he says it's ready so we start eating. My back is to the door, and suddenly the door slides open and this voice says, "Who the damn hell let these *poke'o* boys in my house?" I look at Donkey, he look at me. Then Donkey pushes the plate across the table and Jimmy says, "Oh, that's for me?" So he sits down and the three of us ate. That's how I met Jimmy.

Tony was so buss up. His lips were shrunken, so his mouth was all teeth and it never closed. He was in his thirties when I met him. Jimmy was older, but not as buss up. His hands were damaged, his voice raspy, and lots of scars on his body. I was scared at first but I got used to it and over time I got close to them. They used to have one bedroom at their place and I would stay over and sleep in the bed with Tony. He never messed with me, he wasn't *māhū*, it wasn't like that. He was just really nice.

Later on we started seeing more Samoans in the settlement. There was this big guy, Faamala Taamu. He was sixteen, but already a huge guy. Bernard got him a job working on the garbage truck. By this time I was working garbage truck, too, for fifty cents an hour. That was so much money to me. Years later when I was doing my storytelling for the prisoners at Hālawa, they laughed when I told them I was making fifty cents an hour. That's what they were making, too.

Four-hundred-eighty patients in Kalaupapa when I was there. Funerals all the time but many I was not aware of. I would hear that some guy died and I would go to the service if I knew about it. If he was Mormon I would know because that was our church, but if he was Catholic or Protestant, we wouldn't know about the funeral. We would be talking about so-and-so and then find out he died last week. Aw, shucks. That's how it was.

There was a lot of drinking in Kalaupapa. A lot. Beer mostly. But only in the evening. People would gather at the bar, and after the bar closed some would take their drinks home. I told you about Fanny? We used to go to Fanny's house when we were younger. He would let us drink and cook for us. I remember one time my friend Ben and I came over.

"Hey, Fanny, what you cooking?" I asked.

"Puppy."

"Poppy, what's that?"

"No. Puppy."

I don't know if he was kidding.

Years later he came to the hospital and they cut off his leg. Diabetes. His room was right across mine so one day I came by.

"How you doing, Fanny?"

"Okay."

"You feeling all right?"

"Okay."

And I'm thinking, "He doesn't sound okay to me."

"Fanny, we go *holoholo*, come on. Don't stay in this room, come on, let's go."

So he's in a wheelchair and I'm behind. I was already blind by this time so if I go into the wall on the left, he tell me go right. If I bump into a table on the right, he say go left. I'm driving and he's directing. And you know how long those buildings are. My room was almost in the end and we went all the way to the other side. As we came outside I could hear these men on the porch. As we came close, these guys looking at us. Somebody says, "Hey, look, a blind guy pushing that wheelchair." And they all laughing at us.

And I bent down and tell Fanny, excuse my language, "Fanny, fuck those bastards. Fuck 'em."

Fanny was just laughing. He was having a good time. I took him all the way to the gate. I took him to the benches where visitors came. I took him to the church, to the school, to the shops, then back to his room.

"Fanny," I said, "I hope now you can sleep. You went see lots of stuff, you going have good dreams." He was a nice guy.

THE POND

I grew up Papakōlea, Hawaiian Homestead Land, which is set aside for Hawaiians since 1921. It's right back of Punchbowl. I grew up there when that place was not even considered the National Cemetery of the Pacific. Was just overgrown with bushes and that was part of our playground.

One day when I was in the second grade the boys all got together and said, "Hey, we make one pond." Eh shoot. So all the boys went down inside Pauoa Stream. Quite often we used to play in the stream and we always got scolded. "Hey, you kids get out of that stream!" *Pilau*, you know what I mean, filthy. Polluted because people whose yards would border that stream all the way up the valley, when they clean yard they would throw all that *'ōpala* into the river. You find dead cat, dead dog, dead duck, dead elephant, dead giraffe, and then of course the stuff come stink, dirty up the water.

Below, we catch crawfish. Find an ol' rusty can, wash 'em, put water inside, make fire, eat 'em up. We never got sick, at least we didn't think so.

So the day we decided to make the pond, the boys carry stone, mud, all kine stuff so we can block up the stream. And we had a good-size pond. Not big enough to dive, but big enough to splash around, jump inside. One side of the bank had this tall monkeypod tree and we hang this rope, swing like Tarzan. Yeehaw! Right in the pond.

Those years they never clean the sides of the stream, so it used to be really overgrown with bushes and stuff like that. Right back of the monkeypod tree was the first-grade building. If you're in the building you couldn't see anything because the bushes was so thick. Not unless you took the time to look between the branches. And I have to tell you we boys swim naked.

So every day after school we go to the stream and swim, go home around three-thirty or four. Because I took care of my kid brother, he had to stay and swim with me. He wasn't against it; he liked to swim too, except quite often my sister waiting for us at Papakōlea bridge and we get it from her.

And then one time I was in the fourth grade, every Friday we had assembly. The teacher says, "Oh, boys and girls, we're in for a special treat today. We're having a special program at the cafetorium." So everybody went. We had to march in line, stomp, stomp, everybody walk, find your regular seat and sit down. They close the blinds, turn off the light. Then, pssssshhh, this light went on and shoot up on the screen.

Turns out one day the teacher had this movie camera and guess what she did? She was looking for Hollywood stars. And so she was patient enough to focus between the leaves and branches when we was swimming. And so, we here sitting in this cafeteria and we don't suspect anything. We hear somebody say, "Oh, look, Makia naked! Sammy boy!"

I don't have to tell you how popular we became. And that's how we became famous in Pauoa School. ✦

Chapter Seven

In 1949, the government closed the school in Kalaupapa and sent us to Oʻahu. They had just opened Hale Mōhalu in Pearl City. Some of the patients thought it was part of a plan to close all of Kalaupapa and we were not happy about it. They sent Pili and me to finish our schooling at this new facility. I didn't want to leave Kalaupapa, I loved it so much already. My buddies were being sent there, too, but our hunting trips into the mountains would be a thing of the past. I wouldn't have gone but Beka said, "Mama would be so proud of you." Damn. She knew how to get to me. That was it. I had to go for Mama.

There were over 300 patients at Hale Mōhalu, which was a former military barracks. There were four buildings in all, three levels. On the first floor, one side was the infirmary, the other side the nurses' offices. The doctor lived on the uppermost floor. We had our classroom in the back part of the lobby of the administration building. Our teacher was recruited from Central Intermediate. Her name was Mae Heaka. She was pretty and oh, what a voice.

Twenty of us in the class, different ages, just like in Kalaupapa. The magic of poetry still held me but I was too lazy to get serious. One time for an assignment I wrote a poem and the teacher yelled at me.

"Where did you get it?"

"I wrote it."

"Where did you get it?!"

"I wrote it!"

I finally convinced her and after that she started to look at me differently, as maybe worthy of her attention. The poem was about the Old Ladies' Cave. Basically it was about Kamehameha the Great coming from the Big Island to Moloka'i. He was conquering and killing people on his way to uniting all the Islands. Back then Kalaupapa wasn't as it is today. Just regular Hawaiians lived there.

The Moloka'i people heard that Kamehameha and his canoes were coming, so they ran and hid, some topside, but the ones who lived in Kalawao knew about these lava tubes. There was one tube that went out from the peninsula, off to the left. It goes down deep like a cave and you can hide underneath the surface of the land. They called it Old Ladies' Cave because when Kamehameha came he couldn't find any Hawaiians. He went around the peninsula and saw these two old ladies sitting at the mouth of the cave. They were cleaning their hair, probably looking for 'ukus. Then Kamehameha knew where the Hawaiians were hiding. He found the opening of the cave and he and his men went in and slaughtered everyone. The end. So, you know, it wasn't a happy poem, but the teacher took me seriously after I wrote it. I don't know where it is now.

At Pearl City my parents could come and visit us during the school year. They came a number of times. One day my mother said that my brother Bill had gotten married to another patient in Kalaupapa. I said, "Oh, yeah? To who?" And she told me and I said, "Oh, no." By my reaction she knew something was wrong. I didn't want to tell her this woman had a reputation of being with a lot of guys. Anyway, Bill eventually left her.

Tony Davidson got married, too, I hear—to another patient. That's all there was, yeah? That's the thing about Kalaupapa. So many patients married a lot of times because our world was so small. We only knew each other, felt safe around each other, and so somebody would end up marrying somebody, who used to be married to so-and-so, and before that, married to somebody's ex. Stuff like that. I never saw Tony again. He died when Pili and I were at Hale Mōhalu.

People tried not to have babies, but when they did, the infants would be removed and sent to relatives. They couldn't take the chance that the babies would get the disease. So there were children who grew up on the outside never knowing their true parents.

Beka and Johnny had another kid, a daughter named Derna. She was taken away to be raised by my parents, who were already taking care of her other daughters, Olga and Tweetie. Eventually Beka and Johnny split up, which was too bad 'cause none of the older guys would pick on me when Johnny was around.

In the summer Pili and I would go back to Kalaupapa, which I considered my real home. One summer I decided to introduce Beka to Clarence Tanabe, one of the nonpatient workers from topside. I invited him over with a plan in my head. Sure enough, they got along right away and later married.

At this time the laws were changing about leprosy. The doctors would take snips from us now and then and if the test came back negative one, two, three times, you were "deactivated" and you could leave the settlement. Beka was able to move topside Moloka'i with Clarence. That's where she finally got to see her daughters after all those years. I was not there, but I bet it was great.

There was a construction company fixing the Quonset huts in Kalaupapa. Bill was deactivated and got hired doing some work with them. When the job was done the contractors went back to Maui and Bill went with them.

Pili was also deactivated so he left high school before graduating. He wanted to learn welding. He was training across the old cannery in Iwilei on O'ahu. I was happy for him. His good hands made it possible for him to become a welder.

One time us Pearl City patients went out to see a parade. We were on an open flatbed truck parked across the library. We were watching and waving and here comes this band on the back of a truck. There was my kid brother, playing the alto horn. Oh, it hit me so hard. I was so proud of him. I thought, "How gutsy, to be so exposed to the public like that." A part of me wished I could do that.

Pili was out for three years and then he reactivated.

I stayed at Hale Mōhalu for three years until I graduated, but not just for school. There was this girl patient who came in from

Kaua'i. I was so shy but slowly I got to know her and we fell in love. Ivy and I decided to go back to Kalaupapa together to get married. We were both so young, only eighteen and twenty-two.

We were together for only five years. I'm embarrassed about this. What happened is that I knew this Filipino guy named Ronnie who played music and could sing. I invited him to stay with us in Kalaupapa for a while. Our house was small so he slept on the couch. I didn't think that it would impose on her.

Plus there was this woman up at Bishop Home who was a real gossip. Ivy came home one day and said there was talk that Ronnie had raped someone. I got so goddamned angry. "Why the heck you talk like that about my friend?" We argued. I lost control. I slapped her. She ran out of the house to the neighbor's. I felt so bad that I handled it that way. I was so ashamed. Ivy moved into Bishop Home a few days later. I drove up there and called to her, but nothing. I wanted to apologize but it was too late. A week later I was at the bar and she came by to tell me she was seeing someone else. That was that.

It was not a good time for me. I drank. A lot. One day I woke up and I couldn't see out of my right eye. It was that sudden. I went to the mirror and tried to look but it was just a blur, like something was blocking my eye. My left eye could see up close, but far away, hard time. I remember looking out the window from my bed and I could make out a bulky shape moving across the window. It was the bus that was taking patients to the Polynesian Cultural Center.

One day I asked the nurse to put my pills in one of those dinky pleated cups so it would be easier for me to take.

"Wassamatta, boy, you blind?"

"No, I jus' cannot see." It sounds funny now, but at the time it made perfect sense. "Blind," to me, meant a permanent condition. They sent me to Queen's Hospital and shortly after removed my right eye. Leprosy blindness in one eye usually means the other eye is going to go, too. My whole world collapsed. This, after the failure of my marriage.

I remembered how at Hale Mōhalu the blind people would

stay in their rooms. Nobody wanted to end up in the Blind Ward. For some patients that was the result of having the disease. Before Kalaupapa I had seen only two blind people in my life, a black man and a Hawaiian man. They were both hanging around Fort Street Mall around the Kress Store. The Hawaiian man, he had a stand with magazines, newspapers, and I forget what else. Anyway he had a bowl with some money in it. That's it. He just sat there. He ended up in Kalaupapa, no kidding. I forget his name. But he was blind before he went.

The black man was the other one. You know the Fair Department Store? Fort and Beretania by the Catholic chapel, right across the ʻEwa side of Fort Street. It was almost a whole block, that store, sold clothes and that kind stuff. By the Fair Department was a stairway that went down below the road, and underneath that building they have a bar, and the servicemen during the war, some of them would end up in that bar. Right outside, this big black man was standing with a bunch of newspapers under one arm and one coin changer on his waist. So he's standing on one side of the wall when I pass by. I'm coming from Liberty Theater to meet my brother George. On the way back he's on the other side of the wall. Those were the two blind men I saw. I didn't feel sorry for them. I thought they were fabulous, willing to stand out there, make a living.

The Hawaiian guy, when he came to Kalaupapa I asked him about his bowl, if he had a hard time keeping people from, you know, stealing his money. Because when I was passing him that's what I thought, "Oh, so easy for someone to steal." Of course, I didn't, but anybody could have. He said no, but one time this guy says, "I putting in this twenty and taking my change." And the blind guy says okay. But when he met up with his friend he ask, "Is there a twenty in there?" And the friend say no, so all the guy did was take money from him. Son of a bitch. I was mad but at the same time I'm thinking, "How dumb to sit like that with a bowl open. The smart ones wouldn't do that." He just trusted. So sad, but how dumb.

All these memories came back to me now that I was one

of them. I was not going to be like those blind guys who stayed in their beds. One time Pili took me to see this guy Sammy in the Blind Ward. Sammy had a guitar and he was composing "Sunset of Kalaupapa."

Why must you leave so soon, my dear?
Fills my heart with tears.
With you I have found my only happiness
And how my heart is filled with gladness …

Oh, shucks, I forget the rest.

As the sight in my left eye continued to fail, I did what I could to stay out of the Blind Ward. To me it represented another kind of prison. So I pretended I could still see. I counted steps, I memorized the pathways. I looked in the direction of the people talking to me, like I was seeing them. When the docta' made his rounds and asked me how I was doing I always answered, "Top shape, Docta'!"

But you can hide something like that only so long. The toughest part was having to tell my parents. Finally I called them.

"Mama?"

"Yes, son."

"Can you guys come down? I have something to say."

"Yes, son."

I was nervous when they came to the hospital. I didn't know how they would take it. The last thing I wanted to do was to cause them more grief. My Dad sat at the end of the bed, near my feet. Mama was next to me, rubbing my hands. And now I'm thinking, "They already know. They're acting different. Somebody must have told them."

"Mama, I'm blind."

"Yes, son."

"Did you hear me, Mama? I'm blind."

"Yes, son."

I could hear my Dad sniffling. Mama just sat there rubbing my hands harder and harder. I don't know if she had any tears left. They wanted to be strong for me.

After that I was transferred to the Blind Ward at Hale Mōhalu. Ironically, I had been deactivated, but there was nowhere to go. My parents couldn't take care of a blind person so I decided to stay in the ward. Before settling in, there was something I knew I had to do. I went back to Kalaupapa to establish residency.

See, these guys who were deactivated and went out neva' think about having some place to come back to. You can live outside but sometimes it doesn't work out. Sometimes you get reactivated. Sometimes you just miss the place you grew up in. I wanted to keep a home in Kalaupapa, even if I wasn't living there very often. That was important to me. This was the right of every Kalaupapa patient.

No new patients were coming to Kalaupapa and the ones there were getting older and dying, leaving their houses vacant. The government gave me choices, so I took this house in Bayview, the one I still have today. The occupants had just passed away and the house became available.

At Hale Mōhalu I stayed indoors mostly. I had to accept the fact that I was a blind man. The first thing I did was buy a stereo, the next thing a TV, and weights. I listened to music and lifted weights. At that time they would bring my food tray to me so I didn't need to leave the room except to go to the bathroom down the hall. I'm not a part of the community. I just do my own thing, you know. That's the way I wanted it. My world became even smaller. I couldn't even learn Braille because I had no fingers with which to learn it.

Not everyone on the Blind Ward staff knew how to handle us. They would come by my table and say, "Here."

"Here what?"

"I give this to you."

"Where? What?" Stuff like that.

Then one day I decided I had to go out on my own. I had this goal, just truck around the whole compound, just for my own sake, to see if I could do it. What harm would it do? I waited until I heard the nurse go down the hall and I walked out the back door.

And then I saw these bright flashes and heard this *boom, boom*! I was so scared. I jumped back in my room, ran under the covers. It was just thunder and lightning.

Eventually I built up the courage to just walk out the building. I didn't care what anybody thought. The nurses would be looking for me, calling for me. Counting steps, I would walk down this road that would take me to the front gate. One time I hear this voice, "Son …" This was the lady we called Ma, Mrs. Aki, one of the nurses. She called me son. As soon as I heard her voice I take off for the gate and hide because I knew tall plants were there that I could duck under. And she sees me running and walks over to me. "Son, what are you doing? It's dark now. You can fall and get hurt." Of course, dark, light, to me, no difference. She caught me and took me back to my room. And so I had this reputation for being a rascal.

You know, I'm blind but the images are still in there. Light and movement, I see. It's like BBs or small seeds, a whole mess of them, and they move around. And colors, bright light. More on my right side, where the eye is gone, than on the left side. No kidding. All the colors. It's like a big smear. In the background is dark green, up front, brown and light silvery shades and they all move, in little balls. And when I cough I see flashes of bright, bright light, all beaded and moving. People don't believe me but I can see these things. [Note: Phantom eye syndrome: visual hallucinations can persist after the removal of an eye. The visual cortex, the portion of the brain that processes visual activity, can still register stimuli, creating the illusion of shape and color.]

Later on, my friend Eddie gave me a cane. It was someone else's left behind. I didn't know how to use it. I would bang, bang, and feel my way out of the hospital, bang, bang, follow the sidewalk, listen to traffic, bang, bang against anything in my way. Then nothing could stop me. Oh, I gave them problems, the nurses. I would walk right out into the street.

In the back of the building there was a bridge, a kind of walkway that went over a dry riverbed that came down from

Waimano Home. On the other side of the bridge was a big field where we used to play when we were in the Pearl City school. I remembered the way it looked. At night I would count the steps and walk right out of the building. I would make my way to this bridge where I would listen to the sounds around me, the traffic, the birds. I wanted to be in the real world. I would walk to the other side of the bridge, just to feel what it was like, you know, to be free in this open field. And if it rained the night before I would stand on the bridge and listen to the water rush through the riverbed and out the valley, on its way to the sea.

THE GIANT *HE'E* OF KALAUPAPA

My brother and I would go fishing in Kalaupapa. We went to Ocean View, right by the cattle guard. We would go down to the beach, into the water. We were going for *wana*, the porcupine urchin. After a while I looked for Pili and he was going around the bend. So I followed. Around the corner suddenly I saw a wall of *limu*, seaweed, about seven or eight feet high. I never seen a wall of *limu* so high. And when a wave came, the *limu* would sway back and forth. As I tried to get around the bend my spear whacked the wall and it just fell apart. I never seen that before. It was a *he'e*, a giant octopus, on the rocks and the *limu* was stuck to it. I looked down at the pile of rocks and I see these two eyes looking back at me. (At this part of the story I'm talking softer and softer, and the kids are getting very quiet.)

I put my spear between the eyes and *push*! *Woooo*! (The kids jump!) Now when you spear a *he'e*, you don't just pull it out because it's going to cling to the rocks. You have to shake it and that agitates the *he'e* and it lets go and hangs onto the spear and then you can pull it all out. I was happy because it was a big *he'e*.

You know, with this disease I have, you lose feeling. I'm holding the spear and walking back to the beach. What I didn't know is that the *he'e* is on the spear and slowly making its way down to my arm. Then it wraps itself around my arm but I couldn't feel it. I only felt it when it wrapped itself around my neck. (I'm talking softer and softer.) And then it suddenly reaches and pulls out my eye! You don't believe me? For those who are scared, don't look. If you're not scared, enjoy the view. I'm going to count ooooooone, twooooooo, *three*! (And I yank off my glasses and they see I'm missing an eye. They scream and scream. After I told that story at a couple schools my wife Ann said maybe I shouldn't tell it anymore.) ✦

Chapter Eight

Everything changed when Hale Mōhalu hired this lady. We had lost our athletic guy in charge of games. George Malama, you heard of him? Used to play basketball for UH [University of Hawai'i]. When he left, this lady came for a job as a physical therapist. We already had one so she took George's job. This lady, the first time she saw me she asked if I wanted to go back to school.

"Nah."

"Why not?"

"New math, new English, I don't know what the heck those things are."

"Have you ever written a story?"

"Nah, I don't know how to write."

"If you could, what would you write about?"

"Oh, I dunno, maybe Hawaiian fairy tale, you know, the kind talking animals and birds and stuff like that."

And then this article in the newspaper came out. This physical therapist lady came running to my room. I was lifting weights at the time. "Elroy, I want to read you this article," she said. There was this writing contest run by some blind people, they had a *hui*, this group of people in Oregon. She read me the winning entry, something about travels, and I listened and thought, "Hell, that's no big deal. I can write better stories than that." So she made me promise to come to her office every day from eight to ten and I would dictate to her. I never dictated to anybody before so I didn't know what the heck to do. I went there and she and I would just talk.

Every day I went and in two weeks and two days I was finished. The story was about a pig named Kāpulu, and you know how pigs are, they're dirty and that's what *kāpulu* means. It sounds like an ancient legend but I made it up. She sent it in. That was December '69. I didn't think about it again until the next year when we found out I won. My world was suddenly bigger.

That's how Hoʻopono Rehabilitation Center found out about me and the people there contacted Hale Mōhalu. They thought they could work with me. So then I had a choice to attend the Rehab Center at Kuakini and Liliha. I took it. I was the first patient from Kalaupapa to get blind training. Hoʻopono opened doors for me. I learned how to use a cane, how to catch bus, how to get a cab, how to work with a guide dog.

A guy came up from Australia to train me with my first dog, Kirin. I had that dog for about a year, then Inka Blue, whose full name was Inka Blue Kalealoha Malo Incorporated Esquire Junior the Third. And the last, Ka Makaʻimiloa, which means The Far-Searching Eyes. They eventually retired him, so I gave him to one of the nurses. I didn't get another because by that time I couldn't walk.

THE LEGEND OF KĀPULU

There was once an *aliʻi*, a chief, who had a pig for a pet. His name was Kāpulu, meaning "dirty" in Hawaiian. He was a very spoiled pig. He had his own attendants. He was fed from an *ʻeke*, a basket, with many delicacies. He ate them all up. In the evening he would be loose in the taro and banana patches, squealing.

At this time it was *makahiki*, when the whole village prepared for war games, sort of an Olympics. They had contests in spears, clubs, stones. The day would start with the conch-shell blowing. It could be heard through the whole valley. Then a chant. Then a very pretty girl would start dancing.

Kāpulu was eating and he looked over the rim of the bowl and his eyes got very wide. He just stared. He had never seen such a beautiful woman. He got all excited and ran up to her and knocked her over.

The *ali'i* was so mad, he banished Kāpulu from the village. Kāpulu was so ashamed. His ears hung down and he walked into the forest. He was feeling so bad.

There he meets a mysterious old man. Kāpulu explains what happened and the old man tells him he can use magic to change him into a human and he can go back to the village and challenge the *ali'i* for the heart of the beautiful woman.

"Though I can change you on the outside," he says, "only you can change yourself inside."

So in the middle of the *makahiki*, here comes this straggly stranger walking in. Everybody looks at him. He starts participating in all the games and every time the two winners are the *ali'i* and this stranger.

Kāpulu wanted to get even. Since they were the final winners, they were to challenge each other. When the *ali'i* went to get his club, Kāpulu charged him. The *ali'i* saw him coming and sideswiped him. Kāpulu fell and went squealing and that's when the *ali'i* found out who it was. He then banned Kāpulu from Hawai'i forever. And Kāpulu never returned. The moral of the story is that bad habits stay with you until you make the effort to change.

After winning the contest I went back to Kalaupapa, and my friend Ben, who was also blind, says, "Eh, that Ho'opono, you think they can do something for me?" I said, "Yeah, brah, call 'em." And he did and they brought him to one of their new cottages in Nu'uanu. There were two rooms and had one guy to each. Ho'opono had hired this new lady who was in charge of the cottage. Anyway, when Ben came back Kalaupapa she came with him, ha ha. They fell in love and Ho'opono lost her.

It was also at this time they sent me Queen's Hospital for whatever, I can't recall. I met this young lady who was very attentive to me, a nurses' aide. When she was taking care of me I was just talking story with her, about Kalaupapa, about growing up. She was good company. She was always with me. Her name was Sharon. When I went back to Hale Mōhalu she asked the head nurse for permission to take me downstairs to the van. I said goodbye to her and I said, "You know, Sharon, you're so nice. Thank you for being such an angel." And I thought that was it.

Back at Hale Mōhalu I was lying on my bed, listening to TV, and the attending nurse comes, stands by the door and says kind of mean like, "Elroy, you have a visitor." And I thought, "What the hell did I do? Why she yelling at me like that for?" I got up, sitting on my bed, turned off the TV and got ready to change my clothes because I was in pj's. And then this soft voice comes in. "Hi, 'Kia." She comes into the room. I'm thinking, "Who's this?" And she kiss me on the cheek. I say, "Who's this?" And she says, "Sharon." Sharon? Oh, God. Then I thought, "How the heck she know where I am?" And that's how it started.

After that she came regularly to visit, take me out, we went to eat. I started telephoning her. And then her younger sister finally told her parents. I'm talking to Sharon on the telephone and I hear this female voice.

"Hang up that phone. Shut up already, hang up that damn phone."

"Oh," I told her, "I don't want to cause you any problem, Sharon, please hang up." She was crying. Oh, damn. I called back later and the father picked up the telephone.

"Hello, this is Sharon's friend. My name is Makia."

"You know, Makia, my daughter just got her first job, she's now earning something. I just want her to be safe."

"I want that for her, too."

I wasn't planning anything in particular. No agenda. After that Sharon still came to see me, she insisted. I was slowly falling in love, but I was afraid because of, you know, my history. But Sharon seemed to like me for who I was. It took awhile, but her family came to accept me. They could see I would not harm her. So Sharon and I got married at my parents' place in Papakōlea, under the trees. Her parents came, and her sisters. We had a *pā'ina* up there, her family and mine.

Sharon and I had our own apartment in Makiki. I was getting a twenty-five-dollar stipend every quarter from the state and Sharon was working at Queen's, making only about $200-something a month. Then she became a licensed practical nurse at Tripler Hospital, making $600 a month, which was good money back then.

A lot of things were changing. The Rehab Center encouraged me to go back to school. They had me take the SAT and I guess I passed, so I got into the University of Hawai'i with their help. The university! I never thought I would go to college. I didn't have any dreams like that. I remember one time at Pauoa Elementary my cousin was so excited because he was going to take the test to go Kamehameha Schools. I thought to myself, "I could take that test, too. I'm pure Hawaiian, I could get in, wouldn't that be great? Mama would be so proud." I ran home and told her I wanted to take the test, and I will never forget this. She looked at me and said, "Kawānanakoa [Intermediate School] good enough for you." I was so hurt hearing those words but I understand now why she said them. She wasn't trying to be mean. She didn't want me to hope for something and be disappointed. My Mama, her generation grew up differently. You know your place. You grow up, grow taro, mind your own business. She didn't want me to face failure, so no try in the first place, yeah?

But me, I was ready. University of Hawai'i!

THE MALO TURTLE

My Daddy, one day he come home with a turtle, one good-size sea turtle.

"Daddy, what you going do with the turtle?"

"We going keep 'em for now."

You see, our family didn't know how to clean turtle. He did say, in time, if we could find someone who could clean turtle maybe we eat the turtle. Boy, my eyeball went pop out when I look this shaka pet, but all the turtle would do is bob the head and flap the wing. I was so fascinated by this turtle. I would sit for hours and just watch.

Our house, we had a place where Mama had her washing

machine, and that's where we keep the turtle. I put the turtle inside the hopper where Mama rinse the clothes, so I fill up with water, but the turtle too big for the hopper. The only way it could stay was sideways, so I put the head under water, but I realized the turtle had to breathe, so every time I put him in the water, I put him back out, and he go "ppppp," blow the air, and me, I found that so fascinating.

The kids in the neighborhood would pass outside. "Makia, what you doing?" "Oh, nothing." 'Cause I no like them come near my turtle.

Bum by they see me carrying this strange thing.

"What that?"

"That's my new pet."

"What kind pet that?"

"One turtle."

"I can touch 'em?"

"Uh-uh, you no can touch."

"I give you candy."

"Oh, what kind candy?"

"If good kind, okay, only one touch."

The whole neighborhood was excited. "Eh, you heard Makia get one turtle?" The kids would all stand outside the road and look down inside.

Sometimes I put the turtle on this place where we clean taro, and I shoot it with the hose. Oh, the turtle would go flapping the wings, the water sprinkling its face.

I was always proud I had a secret because I had a fabulous pet, but I couldn't keep it to myself. And I started talking about this pet. Finally my teacher heard about it.

"How come you children are so restless?"

"Oh, Elroy has a pet turtle."

"Oh, really?"

As the days pass by, all the students, each in turn, started to talk about their pets. Everybody had cats, had dogs, some had birds, horses, 'cause up in Pauoa they had horses and cows in those days. But nobody had an interesting pet like mine.

One day the teacher wanted the kids to come up to the house

and look my turtle but I was trying to plan out how I was going charge each one, how much candy I going get just to watch my turtle.

One day when I got into the kitchen I heard Daddy say, "I think we gotta let go this turtle. This turtle not eating, going *make*." I said, "No, Daddy, not my turtle, that's mine, that's my friend, you not going let him go." And my Mama says, "Son, we have to let this turtle go, it's going to die. What would you rather have, the turtle *make* or go free and live?" And I started to cry. I couldn't sleep that night.

The next morning on the way to the taro patch, I carried the turtle to the station wagon and I sat in the last seat with Uncle Moku. And every now and then I reach and touch the turtle. But you see, that morning, my Daddy did a special thing. He got bright red paint and painted our name on the back of this turtle. Malo, PH 65905, only five numbers at the time.

And we going down and I cry, and every now and then I touch that turtle. "I love you, turtle." We drove all the way down to Kualoa Beach Park, just past, by the sandy beach. Daddy pull by the side. And more I started to panic, so I was ready to stamp my feet, bang the car, get a tantrum. I was so broken up. I heard Daddy get out of the car, walk to the back part. I neva' like look at my Daddy, I neva' like look at the turtle and then my Daddy says, "Makia, you like help Daddy carry the turtle down to the beach?" I couldn't talk. My heart overflowed with sadness. I went behind the car and pick up the turtle and in my heart I'm wishing the turtle all the love I could give him.

Walking in the sand, and that turtle heavy, you know, I stumble and Daddy say, "Son, you like help?" "No, I can." In the meantime the turtle is flapping, coming to the edge of the water, I had to drop him, was too heavy. And then he could smell that sea air and that turtle started to flap more vigorously, paddling and paddling and gradually pulled itself into the water, and it came up "ppppp," then dove and each time he came out, can see that bright red spot, Malo PH 65905.

So the last I saw my turtle, as he crested way out, our name was just a red splotch on its back and then he disappeared from my life forever. ◆

Chapter Nine

I was excited. This was my introduction to a new world. You know the Office of Kōkua? I would go there first and an aide would be assigned to help me, take me to classes, get settled. Nice guys, we called them the Nerds. They helped the disabled students on campus although the aim was always to get us to do things on our own. So you know, I learned the pathways and where the buildings were. After a while classmates would see me going to class and they would offer me a hand. I made friends, went with them *holoholo* after school. Two of my best college friends are still my buddies, Gordon and Bill. Bill went into the Peace Corps and went to Malaysia. Years later a woman he met in Malaysia moved to Kaua'i. They hooked up again and got married. They come visit me at Hale Mōhalu maybe twice a year. Good times. People sometimes look back at their lives and remember the good old college days. That's the way it is for me, too.

And oh, the things I learned! I took five classes a day, soaked it all up. Most of the textbooks came in tape cassettes and what I couldn't get at UH, the Library of the Blind would make a recording. Hawaiian language was my major, since I already knew so many words. We spoke English at home but you know pidgin has a lot of Hawaiian in it. For some reason languages came easy. I took four years Hawaiian, got my bachelor's degree in it. I took one year German and one year Spanish, too. The war movies had a lot of words like *fräulein* and *danke* so it was familiar. And the westerns had Spanish words like *riata*. Also comics. You be surprised how much you can learn from comics, the way they spell words. I discovered that once you know one language you had a good idea where to place the words in a sentence in other languages, the grammar. The only thing I needed help with was the pronunciation. I had good grades, mostly As and Bs.

I loved all my classes but I had trouble with math, 'cause you know, I cannot see the numbers. Creative writing was so good because I was already writing but I could see how to organize the words, how other people considered good writers go about doing it. At Ho'opono they help me memorize *Strunk's English Grammar Digest*. As I said, my world was opening up.

Pretty soon people got used to seeing me on campus. I made a lot of friends, but not everyone could handle the fact this guy who had leprosy was sitting in the classroom. On the first day of my Spanish class this lady instructor is talking, going on and on. I say, "Excuse me, can I ask a question?" She didn't respond for the longest time. Then she starts talking again so I ask again, "Can I ask a question?" She didn't say anything. She wasn't going to acknowledge me. I felt bad so at that point I walked out of the classroom. Later, my friends in the class told me she was just staring at me, not saying a word, just staring at me. I think she was scared.

At UH I would run into Bernard Punikai'a now and then. He was taking a law class, one term only. The state was talking about closing Hale Mōhalu and Bernard became the leading activist. He would make the speeches, organize the protests, a real political guy. I would show up now and then. At the library at UH I found the federal government penal system, which is exactly the same system that was used to separate leprosy patients from their families. We were all prisoners. Our trial was the blood test. And if we failed we got sent away.

Things like this got Bernard going. This was not surprising because there was always anger in him. I remember in Kalaupapa there was this guy Piko, a guy you didn't mess with because if you going push, he was going push back. If he wins, you going get hurt bad. Anyway Bernard was running off at the mouth and Piko say, "Eh, Bernard, you watch what you say." And Bernard turn around and say, "Oh, yeah? What you think you going do? You think you can do anything to me? You try it and it's the last thing you do." He was like that, no matter who it was. Not with me, though. Bernard was my mountain-hunting friend. He loved to sing and we would sing a lot together at Kalaupapa.

I asked my counselor if I could take voice, which you think is easy if you've been singing all your life, but let me tell you, there's a lot to learn. When you're fooling around, *kolohe*, you just let it all out, but my instructor at UH had me thinking. She said, "You have a voice box here, in your throat, but the switch is here, in the head. They work together. You have to hit the switch when you want to hit that high note." I could hit high C until I started losing my teeth. You see, I was eating all these lozenges and it wasn't good for my teeth, plus the sugar was not good for my throat. So afterward I cut down on the lozenges and just chewed gum.

Overall, college was a great experience, but it was hard on my marriage. Sharon had a tough work schedule at Tripler. This one time, one of the girls who used to help me get to the classroom, BJ—Barbara Jean—she invited me to this party out at Pearl City for this lady whose daughter was teaching Hawaiian language up at UH. I said okay since Sharon was working that night but I didn't have time to leave Sharon a note that I was going. When I came home she was so upset. She thought I was having an affair, when really, BJ was just a friend. She told me to pack up and leave. I was so sad. I think Sharon knew other people were helping me, taking me places, and she wanted to be the one to do those things for me.

I moved into the dorm and later got an apartment of my own with my stipend and disability money. It was by Punchbowl, which was very close to Papakōlea. I had a woman, a nice lady, who would come and cook and clean for me.

This was a tough time. After all these years, Mama finally caught the disease. She was sent to Hale Mōhalu but stayed in a different ward so we really didn't see each other much. She stayed in the hospital a few months, then they released her and she died soon after.

I don't know when my Dad died. I just remember Beka's girl

Tweetie coming to tell me. She was living with him at our house in Papakōlea. I didn't even go to his funeral because it was over already.

Then Bill passed away on Maui, and Pili died at Queen's. He was at Kalaupapa and started choking in bed so the nuns, they sent him to Queen's to put in a trachea tube. Beka called me and told me they were going to operate. I wanted to talk to him on the phone. He sounded just like Bill because of the trachea tube. Pili died soon after that operation. He was 34. He never married, not even a girl-friend. Shy, like me.

Oh, God, I cried.

People tell me my faith must be strong. To tell you the truth I don't look at it that way. I went to church all those years but I don't hang on my faith. Some things you have to handle on your own. ◆

POEM FOR PILI

Oh Pilipili
Every time I think of you
Sadness of how you went.

I was so proud, the way you
Walked out and worked for a living

Oh Pilipili
I miss you. I love you.
I know you are watching me,
My brother.

Chapter Ten

I t took me seven years to get my degree, then I continued at UH to get my teaching certificate. Meanwhile I was hired to tutor three guys in Hawaiian language. It was fun. I took the approach, match the pidgin because everyone knew pidgin. There was an opening at UH for an instructor in first-year Hawaiian language. I applied and so did a gal I knew, who had a pretty good chance. I won out. She became my assistant. I taught for two years.

In the classroom I tried my best. I think the students liked me, but if there was someone who didn't, it was not my problem. New words, I would usually have the assistant write it on the blackboard, but one day I decided I would write it myself. Make these guys awestruck. I was full of confidence. I reached for the chalk. The thing fell on the floor and my whole world fell with it. In my mind I could see me reach for the chalk and the chalk would keep rolling and my hands couldn't grip it. I saw this as clearly as if it was actually happening. "The students going laugh at me," I thought. I couldn't bear it. I stood up and said to the assistant, "You take over. I quit."

I went back to my apartment and just stayed there. For seven months. I don't know why I was so depressed. Maybe it all hit me at one time, this realization of my limitations. Maybe I was getting too confident. I was thinking I could do anything, when in fact, I could not. It hits you hard.

Now I had time to go back to Kalaupapa now and then, mostly to go swimming. I would go out far in the bay and then yell to hear the echo. From the echo bouncing off the mountains I would know which was the way to the shore.

When I was there one time they were putting on this show about Mother Marianne, one of the nuns that came over to carry on Father Damien's work after he died. I played a patient, no stretch, yeah? From that experience I grew to believe in myself again. I didn't know what life had in store for me, but I was being asked more and more to tell stories. Legends of Old Hawai'i, the ones I grew up knowing, as well as stories about my own life: my childhood in Papakōlea, my years in Kalaupapa.

Auntie Nona Beamer was taking a tour to the public schools, she and Vicky Takemine, Christina Cook and Leo Akana. She asked me to join them as a chanter. I told her, "I'm swollen, I have to take pain pills, I'm just not able to do the show." But Auntie had this way that when you tell her no, she won't hang up, she keep talking. By the time I hang up I said, "Okay, Auntie, I see you soon." Afterward I think, "God fun it, how the hell did I change my mind?"

We did Hawaiian legends, dance. I was dressed up in a *malo* and cape. We went to schools and meetings on O'ahu, Kaua'i, Lāna'i, Maui, Big Island, too. I went to Guam with my friend Jeff Gere to tell stories at this festival. At this event there was this lady giving tattoos. I told Jeff, "Eh, I'm going to get me a tattoo." But I didn't know what kind. And then I thought about it, a shark with a mouth open. It's in the middle of my back. I don't know if anybody else thought about that kind of tattoo. I mean, I seen it before, but not the same. The lady was very careful, took about forty-five minutes. It didn't hurt because, you know, most my body cannot feel. I was scared, though. It was all for free. She wouldn't take any money from me. Fabulous.

And then Auntie Nona started doing the Elderhostel program. We would go to the UH dorms where the Elderhostel tourists were staying, right down by East-West Center, the Gateway Building toward the quarry. During the summer it was used for classes for Elderhostel. I chanted and talked about whatever. It was then I met Ann.

Courtesy Yodie Noe Mizukami

The Malo family in 1952 (left to right): George, Jr. held by Alma (wife of George, Sr.), William Malo (Makia's father), Beka, Olga (with 'ukulele), Johnny, Tweetie, Murial (David's first wife), Makia, Derna (on David's lap), Mary (Makia's mother), Pu'a (Bill), David, Pu'a's wife Betsy, Pilipili, George Sr. holding Yodie Noe.

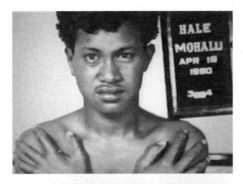
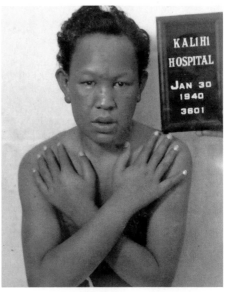

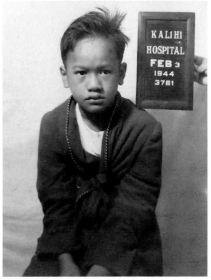

All photos: Hawaiʻi State Department of Health

Kalihi Hospital admittance photos ca. 1940s (clockwise from top): Makia Malo, Bill (Puʻa) Malo, Pilipili (Earl) Malo, Pearl (Beka) Malo and Bernard Punikaiʻa.

Courtesy Yodie Noe Mizukami

Hawai'i State Archives

Top: Sister Frances, a Kalaupapa nun, sits by the "barrier bench." Residents and visitors were only allowed to talk to one another from opposite sides of this barrier.

Above: The original Baldwin Home sits front and center in a 1924 aerial view. On the shoreline just beyond is the U.S. Leprosy Investigation Center.

Courtesy Yodie Noe Mizukami

Party time: dancing with niece Noe in 2008. Left: Makia plays the piano at Hale Mōhalu in Kaimukī. Opposite top: Makia and Ann celebrate at a Kalaupapa New Year's Eve party in 2003. Opposite bottom: Makia's house at Kalaupapa.

Courtesy Yodie Noe Mizukami

Courtesy Yodie Noe Mizukami

Courtesy Richard Miller

Courtesy Yodie Noe Mizukami

Above: Ann and Makia, Kalaupapa, New Year's Eve, 2003. Opposite top: In 2009, Makia takes communion at Father Damien's canonization celebration in Tremelo, Belgium. Opposite bottom: At the Congregation of the Sacred Heart of Jesus and Mary in Leuven, Belgium.

Courtesy Diocese of Honolulu

Courtesy Diocese of Honolulu

Gary Sprinkle

Gary Sprinkle

Top: Pamela Young and Makia at Hale Mōhalu. Above: Makia plays for caregiver and confidant Sheldon Liu.

Ann saw Auntie Nona at one of the programs at the university, like opera show and discussion. Auntie had all these flowers in her hair, all done up, and Ann said she never saw anything like it before. They became friends. And one day Auntie picks me up for our performance and in the car she says, "Oh, you know Ann, don't you?"

"Ann, who dat?"

And after the show Auntie had to go to a birthday party so she asks Ann to drop me off. Ann started talking about these CDs she had about storytelling and would I like to hear them? I said okay, so at her place I listened. It was evening time and Ann says, "I'm going to pick up some dinner, you want?" Some kind of *haole* food, it was. Chicken, fries, pasta, *haole* stuff.

So slowly over those months we were performing, traveling, I was left in Ann's care. She told me about her family, her parents, brother, sisters. The Dad's a millionaire in New England. Ann was an angel, but I didn't see we had anything in common. She was from the Mainland, probably wasn't going to stay here.

Then she told me she really cared for me. She said she knew the kind of person I was, saw the person inside. I'm thinking, "This *wahine*, she playing a joke on me. She not too bright, come Hawai'i and find me."

"Makia, I really like you."

"You nice, too."

"You have a girlfriend? A lady you're close to?"

"I have friends, nothing romantic. I was married before."

She thought about that.

With all I had to cope with I didn't think there was anything there to love. I felt bad for her. I told her. I wasn't being cruel, but I didn't want to hurt her feelings. I wanted her to know, "Look at me, you're out of your head." The place for her was not with me. She was *haole* and she was rich. She didn't have the disease. I was fifty-one. She was in her forties.

But it was tough to say no to Ann. She slowly started to cut the resistance. And we had fun together, joking each other. She thought I was something, but *she* was something. She said she loved me and I gave in. Despite my fears I began to see a life with this woman who was so different from me. That's when we went to the Big Island, to Kīlauea. She planned it to be very special and very private. We stayed at this hotel, the one at the crater. Our room, the floor is at the edge of the crater. She was at the window describing everything to me and I thought, "Kind of spooky, yeah, being at the edge of the crater." She was so caught up in what she saw. This was the first time she had been to the volcano. I could hear the excitement in her voice.

We made our vows there to each other. We said we loved each other. We had our own kind of marriage ceremony. That's how we started our marriage. But still I couldn't believe it. She deserved so much more. I was nervous about intimacy. I was a little shy about making love. In my mind, I think I see myself honestly. I know what I look like. It's something I carry with me all the time, especially when I'm around nonpatients. I wasn't worthy of her. She didn't have any boyfriend before me. But she seemed to enjoy being with me. She would fall asleep after. Me, too.

Ann wanted her folks to know about us. She wrote to her brother so that he could tell the parents. Her brother was so excited. So he went to the parents' house as they were about to leave. So Andy walks in and says, "Wait, wait, sit down, I got this great news." And he started to tell them. He was so happy for Ann, she finally had somebody. The father looked at his wife, stood up, grabbed her, and just walked out of the house, leaving Andy behind.

One day I came home and she talking on the phone.

"Dad, Dad, Makia is here." She hands me the phone.

"Hello, Mr. Grant." There's this pause.

"Makia?"

"Yes?"

"Don't think you're getting one damn red cent of my money! Anything happens to Ann, her money goes to her nieces and nephews."

"Good idea. I think that's very smart."

Another pause.

"You know, Makia, I don't know if you're a nice guy or a damn smart con artist."

And I started to laugh. Ann was happy because she thought her Dad and I were getting along. I told her he called me a con artist, and I said, "Shove his money."

Eventually they accepted me. Ann could be very persuasive. We officially married the following year at our apartment next to 'Iolani School. Ann wanted three different officiants: a Tibetan lama, a Jewish rabbi and a Protestant minister. A psychic once told her she would have an unusual marriage, and that's exactly what it was.

She took me to New York, where there was a reunion of her family, her parents, Mr. and Mrs. Grant, her brother Andy, and her sisters, I forget the names. Mr. Grant was not really nice but I think over time they got used to me.

Ann and I never planned a family, just thought if it happened it happened. But I knew I could never have children—because of The Curse. I told Ann about it and she didn't say much after that. I don't know if she believed me. Mama told me all about it when I was already grown up. It's because of The Curse on the Malo family that I cannot have children.

THE CURSE

When Mama was young her mother would treat her like a slave, take Mama to all the members of the family who had children and Mama had to help them clean up and do whatever. Grandma would take her house to house without any consideration of her feelings. So at age fifteen, Mama got sick and tired of it and ran away.

After three years Grandma found out Mama was on Moloka'i with a family out there. I don't know how she found out. Grandma asked Mama's older brother John to go Moloka'i, bring her home. You know John Kekino, ever heard of him? Anyway, Uncle John went up Moloka'i and found Mama. He brought her to his home in Lā'ie.

In those days, only one store, the Wong family's. When I grew up it was still here, only one store. Mama said nighttime that's where the boys hang out, play all kind games there under the streetlight.

Uncle John was in charge of the telephone exchange. Those days they had exchange, yeah? Mama helped him. One day this man comes over and asks Uncle John if he would hire one of his daughters for this job that was open. Uncle John says too late, cannot, because he already promised the job to another girl. That man left and he was angry.

So the next day Mama is walking along the train tracks, looking for sugar cane that fell off the sugar car. She walking along, she looking one side, she looking other side. All of a sudden somebody pop up in front of her. This man holding a sugar cane stalk out to her. Doesn't say a word, just holding the sugar cane. Mama stopped. She look at the sugar cane, she look at the man. She look at the sugar cane and grab 'em and start biting.

That night she was in the house and wanted to pee so she went outside under the tree. She was crouching and all of a sudden this huge fireball come from above, hit the roof, smash on the roof. Without one sound. Have you ever heard of something like that? *Akualele*, the Hawaiians call it, the Flying God. This is The Curse.

Later on things settle down and Mama is getting ready for sleep. She's taking off her *muʻumuʻu*, lifting it over her head, when it suddenly feels like one big crab, grabbing her around the neck and under her arms, squeezing her. She screams and runs out of the house bare-ass naked, like she possessed, ran into the road, heading to that light in the street in front of the Wong Store.

The boys, they hear this screaming and they spread out but they cannot see her because it's dark. But somebody catches her. Mama told me, "Your Daddy was the fastest." He ran after her, pulled her hair back, lifted her up and carried her back to Uncle John's house. Now Hawaiians know when somebody possessed, the spirit inside cannot stand it when you pull the hair. They scream a sound like you neva' heard before. But my Daddy, he carried her to the house. After that he took care of her for one whole month. And then they married. I asked Mama, "You married somebody you didn't love?" She say, "Love, take care, same thing."

And that is what Mama explained to me why there are only two of her children who had kids. Bill no more, George I died, Stanley died, baby Margaret died, David no more, Pili no more, Beka had girls. She had one boy but he died. George II is the only Malo who has a boy who survived, his son George Jr.

And Uncle John's son Kala dropped dead suddenly while paddling Ala Wai, you remember that? So I knew the chances of me having children were small. I've been with five ladies. Three I married and two was just teenage fooling around. Nobody got pregnant.

And all because that man who was mad at Uncle John went to see a *kahuna*. That *kahuna* is who gave Mama the sugar cane. When she took it that was the "point of contact," you see. Hawaiians believe you must have a point of contact for The Curse to activate.

Once a month I would go back to Kalaupapa to keep residency, take care of business, stay one week, then come back to town. It was a good routine because Ann needed a break now and then from taking care of me. Over the holidays, we would both go to Kalaupapa together for a few days. My house had a bedroom, a kitchen and parlor together, and a bathroom. I bought furniture, some from Honolulu, but not all at one time because I didn't have the money. Ann bought comforters and changed the drapes, little things she changed. It's a very comfortable house. She made it a home.

We had arguments, like any marriage. I can't really say why it worked, it just did. There are so many things I was able to do because of her. We traveled to Belgium for Father Damien's beatification. And to the Glistening Waters Storytelling Festival in New Zealand, and the National Storytelling Festival in Tennessee, and the World Expo in Spain, and to Scotland, where I performed with Kumu Kahua Theatre. I even chanted at the United Nations. And everywhere I told my stories. And Ann would listen. Sometimes I would get paid and I would give the money to Ann. She spent money on me like I was a baby, so when I made money, it was hers.

This is a time I was proud. I was working. I was paying taxes. I could stand tall because I was not on a free ride.

Ann treated me to all kinds of stuff. We went to eat, Hau Tree Lānai, that was my favorite breakfast place. Before that we'd go swimming. When I was in the mood, when I'd be exercising in the water, I'd start singing Hawaiian songs, just blasting toward the ocean. I never thought about anyone hearing me. I was just singing to the ocean. It felt fabulous. All the time I thought Ann was swimming, but she was listening.

She remembered all the stories I was telling about the people who were part of Kalaupapa and Hale Mōhalu, even people at the Rehab Center for the Blind. She wanted to know who they were. And as I would tell my stories she would ask for their phone numbers. This went on for months.

And then it came to my birthday, my first birthday with her. She tells me, "You know, there's a restaurant I found and they play music from the forties."

"Really? Wow, can we go there?"

So she takes me to this place and as we're getting out of the car a man walks by and says, "Hi, Ann." She sort of mumbles something. He kind of snickers and walked away fast. Some kind of message there. I wasn't really paying attention. So she leads me in and it's quiet. As we got up to the steps the music started, this piano playing music from the '40s, Frank Sinatra, Nat King Cole, and I'm thinking, "Wow, this is fabulous."

Then this voice comes up to me. "Oh hi, Uncle." She pulling my shirt and then disappears. "Oh," I thought, "who was that?" As we start walking down the pianist finishes the song and starts playing "Happy Birthday." And I said to Ann, "Oh wow, it's somebody's birthday." Then I realized it was me. Oh God, I almost fell on the floor. Oh man. It wasn't a restaurant. It was a hall across Foodland in Mānoa. It was a church hall and she somehow got permission to use it. Oh gee. About a hundred people, all called up from the phone numbers I gave her or tracked down from the stories I told her.

I was surprised. Every birthday I was surprised. Ann would

set me up every year. She'd say, "Let's have brunch, okay?" And we go to these different places and it's quiet and we sit down and then they all start singing "Happy Birthday." Every time new people, sometimes people we just met. It was something, my birthdays. She fooled me every time.

PEARL HARBOR

One morning when I was about six years old I got up and it was as if no one else was home. As if I was all by myself. So I went and grabbed my agates, my marbles, and went out in the yard. "Gee," I'm thinking, "Where my Daddy? My Mama not around? My brother Pili, he's not around?" And then I heard people walking, a lot of voices heading past our yard, and so I went out the driveway and I saw everybody walking down toward the Papakōlea bridge.

And when I looked down, at the bridge was my Mama and Daddy and my brother Pili. And they were all looking down at Pearl Harbor side. And I remember as I'm walking down toward them there was this huge black smoke billowing up in the air out of Pearl Harbor. And as I was walking down and trying to call my Mama, a plane was coming over Punchbowl and began to strafe because everybody started to run. My folks come running toward me, they grab me, they yank me in the yard, went into our house.

By the end of the day all the men in our household left to help at the harbor. My Daddy, my uncle, one of my brothers who was with the merchant marine. We had other young people who lived with our family and they were *hānai*ed by my folks. They were kids from the neighborhood who had a hard time with their own parents so at least they stayed out of trouble living with us. We had anywhere maybe up to twenty people in our household. We had a huge house, two stories, and these older boys that lived with us, they were like older brothers to me.

But they all left because during those early months of the war all them men were so busy. My Daddy was gone for almost a month. In the home was just Mama, my sister Beka, my brother George, me, and my brother Pili.

We had to carry all the double beds and bring 'em into the kitchen. The doorway so narrow the old-style double bed, you gotta take 'em apart, carry piece by piece. We had four double beds in the kitchen, huge kitchen we had. And the kine floor lamp, that's the only light we had in the house. Those years they stressed had to be absolute dark, no light could escape from any house, so people would paint the windows black, they would hang blankets over the door.

Someone in the neighborhood would be assigned as block warden and he had the authority to arrest you if you were persistent in letting light escape from your house. They went around the neighborhood banging on your door telling you, "The light, the light," and so you had to scramble and make sure no lights escaped.

Our household, all we had was Mama, and things were pretty scary because we never knew where the men were. Our family, we had taro patch so insofar as food our family was all set. But those who depended on the stores for food, they were the ones that really had a hard time.

My Daddy used to buy food by the cases because we had such a large family … canned corned beef, Spam, lunch tongue, pork 'n' beans, Vienna sausage, deviled ham, eggs by the case, rice by the bags when we can get rice. We had all kine foods and we wouldn't just eat anytime. Daddy had the room bar locked so that we wouldn't eat all one day and then tomorrow *oka*, right?

So those years were really hard and in fact the poi factory that used to be on Fourth Street and Kuakini, that line was stretched three, four, five blocks because people waiting for the poi factory to open. I was little bit too young to really appreciate what it was like, you know, because we had our own taro, so we had poi. My Daddy made sure we always had food.

What happened in school, everybody had to carry their gas mask. They were so afraid that gas would be dropped on the population so no matter where you went, even if you went toilet, you gotta carry your gas mask. You even go take a bath you gotta hang your gas mask close by so you can get it on.

In schools, it was almost a daily ritual where you have to practice putting on your gas mask anywhere between three to five seconds. Because you figure that's all before you die. So you look like something from Mars, you know, this gas mask get big kine eye over here, like your face all covered with this rubber stuff and this big can hanging down underneath the chin that would filter the air so you can breathe.

And then they starting to dig up the schoolyards. They put in bomb shelters. Our school we had air-raid rehearsals at least once a week. They'd ring the bell, within so many minutes the classes would have to be in that bomb shelter.

They had places set up for everybody to get inoculation. In our area it was Kawānanakoa Intermediate School. Everybody go down there for injection and oh, man, we not used to getting injection. Da kine tetanus shot, ohhh, feel like you going die, man.

During those years when we used to go to the taro patch we used to pass this place, Kualoa, it's a park now, part of the state's park system. But before that was an airstrip. All the warplanes used to land so if we coming down there they would block the gate, then we can't pass until all the planes either landed or took off. And my brother and I would be on the car, with eye all big, watching all the planes coming in—oh a B-17, oh a B-25, oh B-47. Used to be able to name all the warplanes that used to land.

And they had these huge bunkers with grass and dirt, to put one plane between each in case one plane got destroyed and started to burn it wouldn't affect the other plane in the next bunker. Wherever the planes went during the war time we never knew.

Now, we also had movies in the schoolyard. Almost all the schools, I think the Army took over and they bivouac all their, you know, camp there in the school. Nighttime they had movies, and all the people in the whole valley down by Lusitana, Pacific Heights, from ʻĀlewa Heights, and the other side of Punchbowl, they'd all come down to Pauoa in the evening.

We'd sit with all the servicemen under this big monkeypod tree. The screen hanging down from the monkeypod tree and you gotta sit on the ground so people take goza, you know da kine, straw mat or they take newspaper to sit on top of. They gotta take raincoat too, jacket so that in case rain, we sit down in the rain, you know no go home until the movie *pau*. And you had to make sure your flashlight working okay 'cause when you going home we gotta pass by the graveyard and sooo spooky, man. But that was part of our growing-up years, you know, growing up at Papakōlea. ❧

Chapter Eleven

I was "watching" TV one night and there was a program where several disabled people were talking about how they use computers. Now this was beyond me 'cause to use a computer you need hands. But one of the guys used a Morse-code system. And when I heard that, a light bulb went off. When I lived in Kalaupapa Judge Bell taught me Morse code. He was a real judge who caught the disease. He married Nancy Brady, who's now married to Jimmy Brady. Listening to this program, I thought it might be possible for me to use a computer. I told Ann to come and look at this show. The guy was using some kind of pad to press. There was a long handle with a flat metal piece the size of my palm and you press on top. For the letter A: dot dash, B: dot dit ditto. C: dot ditto dot ditto. It was perfect for someone who couldn't manipulate a keyboard.

Ann waited for the credits and found out who to call. She asked what kind of computer it was and where we could get one. It came from Louisiana State University, which is in Baton Rouge, not far from the Carville Leprosarium. Ann made all the calls and before I knew it, I had a computer from Hoʻopono.

All day I spent at that computer, remembering my stories and writing them down in Morse code in Documents. I tried to remember all the stories, the ones told to me, the ones I told to hundreds of schoolkids on Auntie Nona's tours, the ones I told to strangers when we visited foreign countries.

Ann was always happy when I was writing. She said somebody had to write the stories down so they wouldn't be forgotten. It was important for people to know. My childhood in Papakōlea will never be again, not the way it was. And my journey with this disease is something that never should be again.

MEMORIES

Memories are teased out of their hiding place.
One memory, then another and another.
So many pictures flood my mind
People, places,
Good times, bad times
Sneaking out of the house and into Bishop Home nights.
Trysts down at the pier.
$1.60 lupchong dinners with eggs and rice.
So many fun days with the guys.

A sweet yearning
A good kind of yearning
Is astir now
But my heart aches.
Pili, Ubaff, Donkey.
So many went before me.
Sometimes I wonder
How come I neva' go yet?
Ass luck or what?
But neva' mine!
Das awright.
No give up.
If you can you do.
If no can, *pau* awready.

But as long as you can breathe
You suck up every sweet smell you can.
You taste all the *'ono* kine stuff get,
You listen all the nice sounds
Because when the heartbeat stop

And they put the money
On top the eyeball
Tun tun ta run tun
Too late.
All *pau* awready.

We were so happy, Ann and I. But nothing is forever. That's one of the hard lessons you learn over time. You would think after all I've been through I would get used to it. You would think I had a hard shell around me to keep the sadness away.

In 2008, Ann had these times when she wasn't feeling too good. She would stay in bed, not go outside. Then she hurt her knee, I don't remember how, and she had to go to rehab in Kapolei. She stayed there for a couple weeks and then came home. There was a doctor she would see now and then to get vitamins for me and some medication for her. She had me taking all these vitamins. She was into eating healthy, you know. My brother George's daughter Noe would drive her sometimes. Noe was over the house a lot then, and the two of them would talk with each other all the time, always conferring.

What I didn't know was that Ann was very sick. When they were treating her for her leg they did tests and discovered she had cervical cancer. I don't even know what a cervical is. She didn't want me to know, didn't want me to worry, so she never said anything. She only told Noe.

Ann was away more and more and poor Noe was doing triple duty: bringing organic food to the hospital for Ann, taking care of me and also her own family. Then one day Noe said that Ann had been moved to Hospice. I didn't know what that meant. I just thought it was a different kind of hospital. I didn't know it was like, you know, last time. And still, they didn't tell me, trying to spare me. As I think back maybe a part of me didn't want to ask the questions. You know, how I was brought up, you don't talk about it if it's bad.

Ann never tell me she was hurting or in pain, never complained. Then one night Noe called and said, "Uncle, the people at Hospice called and said Auntie passed away." I said, "What?!" Can you believe that's the first time I realized how sick she was?

We drove to Hospice to say our goodbyes. I told Noe to go in first. I sat in the hall, sniffling. How did it come to this? We had avoided the issue for so long and now we had to face it. She was gone.

Noe came out and led me in. I lied down on the bed with Ann and hugged her, face to face. I told her how much I loved her, what she meant to me. I kissed her. Oh God. Then all of a sudden I feel this hot breath, like someone blowing on me. And I knew she was sending me a sign that she knew I was there, that she heard me.

From the time the doctors found out until the day she died, only six months. Ah, she was a wonderful woman. We spread her ashes over Waiʻanae. ❧

POEM FOR ANN

You were … no, you are
The love of my life.
An angel who swept me off my feet.
My heart is with you
And my soul.

Only now I think of saying
And praying
"Lord, let me be worthy
So I can be with my angel."
My love
My Ann.

Chapter Twelve

I'm alone a lot now. I live at the new Hale Mōhalu in Kaimukī and go back to Kalaupapa now and then but it's not the same. Ann isn't there. I don't sleep in the bed. I sleep in the parlor on the sleeping chair. The bottle of rum I left next to the microwave is still there. Nobody stole it.

My computer blew up a couple times so now I don't have one. But my mind won't take a rest. It's always working, making words out of words. Like, how many words can you make out the letters in "house"? Stuff like that. When I was in Kalaupapa and could still see, crossword puzzles were my thing. I knew that to learn new words you had to read a lot, so I had thirty or forty magazines coming in. I still love to play word games. But now I mostly create situations in my mind. I use pieces of my life and make up these stories. Just daydreams. This is one of them:

My Dad was in the service and he almost got killed. His lieutenant saved his life and my Dad met him again years later, a retired general. The nurse who took care of my Dad, the general married her. Mama had just given birth to me. The general and his wife stopped in Hawai'i to see Daddy. Mama grabbed me and put me in their arms. When they left they took me back with them to Idaho. And I grew up there, their hānai son, away from Hawai'i, away from the disease.

There was a river, and a house. We were on top a mountain, a spot where the Native Americans, the Cree, had their reservation. By the time I was twelve I was chasing animals. I started to catch pheasants and raising them as one raises chickens. I had peacocks and turkeys, all these birds, even deer. I started feeding deer and they got tame from me, also buffalo. When the Cree came down for food they see me doing this and told the chief, who gave us personal use of all this land because I was taking care of the animals.

I was home-taught. My stepmom would teach me. I loved the things they would teach me, outside what any other child would receive. I had books, lots of them. I continued to learn and learn. They wanted to send me to school, a university. And so I went at the age of twelve. There were lots of students there, only whites, so there was a lot of comment seeing someone like me. Of course, I stayed out of everyone's way. Between classes I would be swimming, jogging the fields, studying in the library, working weights in the gym, anything to stay out of the way, try not to aggravate.

One time these guys tried to smart-ass me. They had a golf club, some kind of stick, coming at me and I backed up and laughed. I had this whip of ragged steel in my jacket. (Remember this is all a dream, yeah?) This guy came at me and I whipped him, then this other guy started to run, so I did the same thing.

In this dream I'm not blind, I can see. I can walk, I'm healthy. It's a life I maybe could have had. But I know it's a dream and not possible. Besides, I'm not that brave. When I'm low with nothing to do, I add to the story. I know how it's going to end. Those guys on campus will come to respect me. ❧

THE OWL SONG

The owls are flying, I hear them all crying,
Through the trees, and the
    curtains as they hurry on home,
    with an eye on the sky, and my heart sad and lonely,
I sing who who who.
Who will talk to me, who will answer me,
    who knows why I sing who?
Who knows the reason why I sing this melody,
    who who who.

The soft wind at twilight bestirs the green willows,
>	as they sigh in the woods to the owl's refrain,
>	the tears fill my eyes as I hear the faint echo,
>	of who who who?
Who will come with me, who will go with me,
>	who will stay by my side, will you,
>	who knows the reason why I sing this melody,
>	who who who?

From the mountains and valleys and across the green meadows,
>	come the choir of owls with their sweet lullaby,
I think of how Mama would hold me, and croon, too,
>	who who who?
Who will dream with me, who will fly with me,
>	who would possibly take me home,
>	who knows the reason why I sing this melody,
>	who, who, who?

In the deep of the night, when the concert is over,
I long for the sounds of their beautiful song,
>	though this lullaby holds me in sleep on my pillow,
>	wondering who, who, who?
Who will remember me, who will be touched by me,
>	who will know I loved you?
Who'll know the reason why I sing this lullaby,
>	who, who, who?

Chapter Thirteen

S inging was a part of growing up in Papakōlea. We were always singing, making up songs. But then you had to be careful or people would think you were a *māhū*. There was this guy, a hula teacher, and you'd think he was *māhū*, but he wasn't really, or maybe just a little. He was the only guy who knew how to play the piano in Papakōlea.

I really loved to listen to Frank Sinatra and Roy Rogers. I loved their songs and then Nat King Cole. And there was a fabulous play with great songs. What was the name of it? Oh, yeah, *Oklahoma!* And then the guy who sang "Ol' Man River." Do you remember that song? "It juuust keeps rolling aaaaalong." Oh, so fabulous. Anyway, when I was a kid I decided I wanted to learn how to play the piano, so after school I used to take the bus to Bishop Street, behind the Catholic church. Frank Owens' Studio was there, right around the old Kress store. He's the brother of Harry Owens, you know, the big-band leader.

I had lessons at three-thirty. If the bus neva' come, I would run and run just to get there in time. The thing is, I never practiced. "They're going to call me *māhū*," I thought, so I never practiced. But I learned how to read music.

That really helped me when I took voice lessons at UH, even though I couldn't see the sheet music. Ann Ito was head of the office of the disabled students. She made sure I had everything I needed for all my classes.

I loved the show tunes. Some of those Gene Autry movies, the Roy Rogers movies, they had so many songs I loved. So after I had voice training I came out and had sort of an idea of what to do when you're doing it. When I sing the high notes, I'm all open and not tight. High and full.

Ann would sometimes take Bernard and me to a performance at the old Hawai'i Theatre. Bernard and I both couldn't walk by that time. We sat in the back in our wheelchairs and at the end of every performance the orchestra would strike up "Hawai'i Aloha" and everyone would stand and sing. We would sing up good. I could hit the really high notes, not falsetto, but somewhere between tenor and alto. I sang loud and clear. One time Ann said the conductor turned around and looked at us to see who was singing. Oh, we had a fabulous time singing, Bernard and me.

About this time there was talk about Father Damien being made a saint, and then it happened. I don't mean just happened. It was a long process. So the Catholic diocese asked what patients wanted to go to Europe for the canonization. Of course, I wanted to go, especially because Ann and I went on the first trip for his beatification in 1994. But not just because of that. There were nineteen of us left, at the time. We would be representing the more than 8,000 who were sent to Kalaupapa from the very beginning. Outcasts, and now we were being invited to go to the Vatican. Wow. And the world would know what this man did in Kalaupapa, taking care of us, dying as one of us. I kept telling myself, "You've got to go. You've got to go." For Damien. To honor him.

The doctors, they had other ideas. You see, in my ankle now I have crushed bones. Initially on the outside, but now I'm quite sure the inside is crushed as well. I don't know how the heck it happened. I guess like so many of us, we don't feel, we're not aware of it. The doctors were thinking of amputating my leg up until the week we were supposed to leave. But then here was some kind of alternative aggressive treatment they decided to try. They put my leg in a cast to stabilize it.

It turns out we would be going without Bernard. Some time before the announcement he had a stroke in Kalaupapa. He was sent to Hale Mōhalu so we spent some time together. We talked about old times and all the fun we had as boys in the settlement.

Did you know we were Boy Scouts together? I was Cub Scout outside, but inside Kalaupapa there was a Boy Scout troop and Bernard and I were part of it. Lots of guys. Donkey, the two brothers, I can't remember their names. And Kenzo Seki, he was Da Man. In Kalaupapa there is access to three valleys. The middle one, outside there's a flat area where there was a building, I don't know what it was before. The building was not standing anymore but the lower part was there. No roof, just walls and doorway and that's where we Boy Scouts would go camping. Bernard and me, we just wanted the camping part. That's what I remember about Bernard. And all that singing at the back row of Hawai'i Theatre.

What different paths we took. He never married, although I think there was a lady who spent time with him. His health seemed to be fine at first, but over time he sort of lost his mind. He would forget words and it was hard to talk to him.

Bernard went on the first pilgrimage to Belgium with all of us, and this was one of his major campaigns in life, seeing Damien named a saint. You know the old Bernard, always had to have an issue. After the Hale Mōhalu thing* he dedicated a lot of time to the Damien canonization campaign. He died about seven months before the trip to Rome. Oh, what times we had.

*In 1978, the State Department of Health closed Hale Mōhalu at Pearl City and announced the transfer of patients to a new facility within Lē'ahi Hospital near Kaimukī. Bernard was one of ten patients who protested the transfer. He, patient Clarence Naia, and sixteen supporters were arrested shortly before the buildings were torn down.

FIFTY CENTS ONE HOUR

Eh brah! Bernard!
Remember when you help me get that job?
Fifty Cents One Hour!
You stood up for me.
Man, you da guy with the POW-ah.
Fifty Cents One Hour meant I free!

When Beka tell me go Hale Mōhalu in Pearl City
I say no, Beka, 'cause I making
Fifty Cents One Hour!
I can buy anyt'ing I like.
I went anyway, but t'anks, yeah, Bernard.

I will remember you stood up for me
Got me job working garbage truck, fo'
Fifty Cents One Hour!

Finally I got the green light from the doctors to go to Belgium and they piled us Hale Mōhalu patients in a van to the airport, where we would meet the patients joining us from Kalaupapa. Eleven of us in all, each one with a caretaker. Mine was Sheldon Liu, my social worker and friend.

I was excited and a little scared, I have to admit. Although I had been to Belgium before, this pilgrimage would take us back there, and then on to Rome for the actual canonization with Pope Benedict XVI. This was a longer trip, and I would be doing it without Ann. To tell you the truth I wasn't sure we would be welcome. We were Americans and at the time there were bad feelings toward Americans. I was nervous. Sheldon told me, "No worry," because he was there and he would make sure I would be just fine.

It was nine hours to Newark without stopping on the West Coast. There were 200 people from Hawai'i going on the tour, including Bishop Silva and other priests, but I didn't think us patients were going on the same tour. I thought they were going to drop us off somewhere since most of us were in wheelchairs.

The first morning in Belgium Sheldon and I ventured out. The group was divided into three separate hotels. The tour group, Seawind Travel, wanted to protect us from being bothered by the media, so we were split up in different hotels and different buses. Our hotel was on a cliff near the oceanside. Sheldon and I walked and he described the coastline with the rocks close to the pier and the houses built close to the shore. I thought, "Oh, this is just like Kalaupapa." We passed outdoor cafés, about seven of them. He asked if anything sounded interesting to me and I told him, "Whatever you like I'll go for it." That's how we went to eat every morning. One time I had the paella. Sheldon was talking to the waitress, you know, "Make sure you remove the shells because he's blind," so they brought it and I sat and ate it and I couldn't believe the flavor. I cleaned it up. Every bit. Broke da mouth. That's the only meal I really enjoyed. Some place here in Hawaiʻi makes paella, I heard. Somewhere near Pālama Settlement, around Tamashiro Market.

Afterward we had to go back up to the hotel quick because the bus was waiting for us. I thought, "Where the heck we going?" And then I found out we were part of the tour, seeing everything that everyone was seeing. I guess after so many years as a patient, you naturally think your situation is going to have you separated from the normal tourists.

We were driving around Brussels and Sheldon is describing different things to me. I was just floored. So much history. It was great to be back in Belgium. We had anticipated the cold but it wasn't as cold as last time. That was fifteen years ago. I recall back then, Ann and I went to the Damien Museum and I touched the original altar that was in his church in Kalawao. I felt around there and touched a *kāhili*. I couldn't believe it. How come a church of God has a *kāhili*?

We went to Damien's house in Tremelo and that is where I learned that Damien wasn't supposed to come to Hawaiʻi in the first place. His brother was a priest and he was supposed to go, but he got sick so Damien went in his place.

And then we went to the monastery at Leuven where Damien went to study for the priesthood. His crypt is there. I remembered from the trip before the steps that went below. Ann had taken me and I felt through the hole and touched his coffin. This time when we went there was a service going on in the church one floor up and there was a lot of people talking. Someone came to take me down into the crypt and he left me there. I had this fabulous feeling come over me and I started to chant. Just softly. I opened up my heart. Inside, I felt something was roaring inside, felt so good. When I finished the man came back down.

"Oh, were you praying?"

"No, I was chanting."

"What were you saying in the chant?"

"That's between Damien and me."

On one of the days we all got on the buses and drove and drove. It must have been three hours or so. Remember when we were in that village on the mountaintop? Assisi? I remember reading about that place in intermediate school. The village of St. Francis. Other saints, too, because the place is so holy. Sheldon was describing how the people were able to defend themselves. Because the bad guys were below and the villagers on top. So fantastic. We arrived at the bottom of this hill and in the old days you had to hike up to the village, but since then Assisi got a lot of tourists so the government installed an escalator. That's the only way we could have gone up, us in the wheelchairs. Even so it was rough going because the streets are cobblestone. Bumpy ride.

Several days before the canonization we went to St. Peter's Square really early in the morning for an audience with the pope. From our hotel we got on the buses, then had to wait until the guards opened the ropes to the square. Because the patients were special guests, we went in first. Our group was sitting on the left-hand side, the first row. It was in the shade and some of us got cold, sitting there in our wheelchairs. Then half an hour later this other group comes in front of us. Then another group, so now we're in the fourth row. It didn't matter to me if I was in the first row or fourth row, because the pope, when he came, never got out of the car. We thought maybe an audience meant that he would meet us, but I guess it meant he would drive by and we would be in the audience. He didn't greet anybody individually. All I could think of, "When he passes by, somebody tell him hi for me."

On the day of the actual canonization we came back to St. Peter's Square. The crowd was big and I could sense the excitement.

We thought we would be outside, but it was raining hard the night before and, at the last minute, they decided to hold the ceremony in the basilica. They wheeled us in and you could smell the incense and hear the singing echo. Fabulous.

None of us had to do anything, but Audrey Toguchi and her husband were supposed to do something at the altar. Oh, my gosh. She was the woman cured of cancer by praying to Damien. The Vatican investigated it and declared it a miracle and that's one of the reasons Damien was made a saint. Every day on the trip she would come up to me and say, "How's the movie star?" That's because the media was always following us, asking us questions. She is a terrific woman.

My mind was so full, trying to keep track of everything. My whole body was tingling from the experience. The pope spoke in Italian, or Latin or whatever, but every now and then you could hear him say, "Damiano." We were so proud. Finally. But I couldn't help but feel a little sad because Bernard wasn't there. And Ann. But then again, maybe they were.

Now that we're home I'm kinda sad. I don't know why. Sheldon had bought one of these Damien medallions for me and I always had it on but when I started to take a bath I was scrubbing myself with one of the washcloths from Japan. I didn't know but I tore the thing off. After I was drying up I realized I didn't have the thing on and I asked the nurse to check the bathroom and there it was. ✦

An interview with Hansen's disease patient Bernard Punikai'a and State Department of Health director George Yuen, 1979

Bernard When I was first diagnosed, I was attending school in Honolulu and the nurse sent a note to my mother asking that I be taken to the clinic, which I was. The doctor told her I had leprosy and had to be sent away. I didn't understand, really, the separation, not at that time, but I knew it affected my mother tremendously. She really cried a lot and it was very traumatic. The moment I saw her driving off in a black car, I realized that this was it. It was very hard to continue. I had brothers and sisters and I would never touch them again. In fact, when they came to visit me at Kalihi they sometimes ran through the gate and grabbed me and the guards would yell at them, "Get out, get out, don't touch," so even at that age they start to condition us as to how terrible we are.

Pamela As you look back at what you've gone through as a patient, do you harbor any bitterness?

Bernard Not really. I don't think I'm that kind of person. You begin to accept life the way it comes to you and all of us have had to make these adjustments. You have to adjust to the situation otherwise you go nuts. I have seen individuals who could not take it. You accept because there was nothing else you could do.

Pamela A lot of your work takes you out of Kalaupapa these days.

Bernard The last three years my projects have taken me out of the settlement, taken me to Honolulu, a lot of time in the Hale Mōhalu facility. Hale Mōhalu represents to most of us a stand for freedom, a right to make decisions, to share in decisions that affect our lives. We've tried to tell the authorities.

Pamela George, how do you explain the desire of some patients to hold onto Hale Mōhalu?

George I think it's a matter of nostalgia and being accustomed to an old home. We all have those feelings, but I feel once they move to Lē'ahi (Hospital) and see the new surroundings, they will like it.

Bernard These are guys that make their living as public servants and they forget that we are the people the program is for.

George Who owns the land? That is to me the question now. There's no question the state owns the land. The patients feel it's their land and we don't think so.

Bernard Some patients feel they should not say anything against the state because the state is doing all these good things for us and as such, we should just accept. I don't share that kind of feeling. I feel that the fact is I was taken away at the age of six, incarcerated, when I had committed no crime, but was ill. And my illness was considered a threat to the community so I was tossed away. They fed me, clothed me, but they took away my humanity, they took my dignity, they did not allow me to even make decisions. So after all these years, we say, "Uh-uh."

Epilogue

Swimming. It's something I did almost every day when I was young and healthy. I used to walk from Papakōlea to Waikīkī, then walk back before my parents came home. Took me forty-five minutes. Now it's so humbug. Sometimes Sheldon will take me to the side of the Natatorium in Waikīkī. There's a gal who comes to swim with me, Annette, and she knows there's a special wheelchair the lifeguards are responsible for. I think they keep it near the Kaimana Beach Hotel. Sheldon gets the wheelchair and there's this mat that goes all the way to the sand. Sheldon can push me right into the water. The water is shallow. I can make figure eights in the water.

Oh, this is great. Figure eight outside, twist underneath. The water buoys it. The saltwater is so much better for you, but I can do more exercise in a pool because I can hold on and practice running.

The doctors are concerned about my weight, which is now 347 pounds. I don't get enough exercise. I have this big thing, my stomach. I talked to Dr. [Kalani] Brady when he was here last. I thought since women can have this thing surgically removed, maybe I can. It must be costly. I wonder if the state would do it. I wouldn't have this weight if I could walk around. I can stand and make my way from the wheelchair to my bed but the bones in my ankle are crushed. The doctors say if the pain comes back, off my foot comes. I have to be careful.

I had a trip to Kalaupapa planned for a long time. I thought it was going to be fabulous. I had this plan in my mind I would go swimming every day, going down to the pier, jump in the water. I know I can't really swim now, may just hold on to the pier and kick. This guy Steve, the head of the National Park Service, says, "Yeah, I think you could do it." They had a van with a hoist in the back that they use to take these outboards and lower into the water. I explained to Steve, "That's fine, but I cannot climb my way out of the water because of my left leg, so if they just lower the van I can grab on." He said, "Okay, we try." The head nurse, she didn't even want me to try. She didn't even want me to go to my house by myself. Had to have someone with me all the time. I was really futless, really frustrated.

So all I did was go to the bar in the evenings, around five-thirty till closing, eight o'clock. Eat two drumsticks and one soda. Eat one package Cheetos, spend just enough time to connect with everybody. And even then they only let me go if I had a nurse with me. I was really futless.

So now there's not much reason to go back. Except to be buried. You know, everybody who dies in Kalaupapa is buried. No cremation. Not unless you cremated outside and they bring your ashes back. There's no facility to cremate unless they go down by the garbage dumps, start fire, have a big barbecue, ha!

I want to be buried in Kalaupapa. I want to be next to my brother Pilipili. I'll leave some money for Noe and her family to come for a service, but if they can't they can use the money for themselves. Noe still takes care of me. She keeps me stocked in lozenges and stuff. On holidays I take the Handi-Van to Mākaha where she lives. I know it's hard for her with her kids and her job, but she has taken on the responsibility of making sure I know I still have family.

Bill is buried on Maui and my sister Beka is buried topside Moloka'i in the Homestead Cemetery. Beka's daughter Tweetie now has the family house in Papakōlea, the house we all grew up in.

My parents are buried on O'ahu, I think Lā'ie. That's where the family graveyard was. I know my brother Stanley is buried there. So really, I have a choice. But remembering the things that happened to us, it has to be Kalaupapa.

There were so many fabulous people in my life—my family,

my wife. I'm not a religious person, but I know I'll see them again. All I wanted was them to be proud of me. I was lucky in that I had a chance to go out, to see the world, to experience new things, to be educated. Yes, I wish my life had been different, but still it has been so much better than many of the patients who couldn't go out. I hope I brought some pride to Kalaupapa.

I get asked from time to time how I would want history to remember me. Me? I'd be grateful if people would remember all of us, the 8,000-plus who are dead and the handful of us hanging on to represent the past. We lost so much. I hope in the future people learn from us. This is the lesson: No matter where you are, at what age, life can be hard. Life can take everything away from you in one snap of a finger and it doesn't do you any good to sit there and whine about it. Take that cane and bang, bang your way around your problems. I have my memories. I have my stories. ❧

Talk Story Kalaupapa

More than three decades ago I began a series of television reports on the people of Kalaupapa. It was a volatile time, when the uncertainty of the settlement and relocation of patients to Hale Mōhalu in Pearl City were in the headlines daily. Many of the patients I interviewed have since died. I think it's important to share their words here, to bring more color into the canvas of old Kalaupapa painted by Makia's words.

—*Pamela Young*

Alice Chang Kamaka
1906–2000

Alice was sent to Kalaupapa in 1919. When she arrived, Brother Joseph Dutton, who worked with Father Damien, was still caring for patients. After Brother Joseph's death, Alice was given Father Damien's spectacles, which she kept in their case in her kitchen. The glasses were donated to the Damien Museum after her death.

Alice My family was worried for me. You know Chinese, they scared of lepers, yeah? Oooh, one in the family is disgrace. This is what I understood. When I was eight my mother see this hand started to cripple, the fingers, yeah? To me was cute, like one flower. I say, "Eh, Ma, cute, yeah?" She look at me with the eyes full of tears.

Pamela Did your family shun you?

Alice Some of them. I was too happy-go-lucky to think of these junks. Everything was fun to me. I no think of these things.

Pamela What do you remember of your first husband?

Alice Nice-looking Chinese-Hawaiian. Selfish. Very selfish.

Pamela And number two?

Alice A drunkard. We never get along.

Pamela And number three?

Alice Number three we got along real nice. Fatherly kine of, talk to me like sensible.

Pamela And number four?

Alice Number four was very good to me but still cannot beat number three. I never kill him. He killed himself from drinking, drinking. They don't listen docta'. I drink but not much. People come visit, you talk story, drink beer. Two, three bottles is enough for me.

Pamela Were all your husbands patients?

Alice Yeah, all patients, what else was there? Clean guys, only one was lumpy, lumpy swollen.

Pamela You going to get married again?

Alice Now? I gotta find a sugar daddy. You can find one for me?

Pamela Sounds like it was easy to find husbands.

Alice Easy, you telling me. Too many looking for wives, not so many wahine, so natural easy to find one man, yeah? I had a lot of fun with those gentlemen. "Come on, Alice, let's go horseback riding." I jump on the horse, me in the saddle, the guy in the back. I have a lot of fun with the boys. Now I'm alone, watch TV, sit down write some stupid letter, all those things. So days go by.

Pamela Were the old times better?

Alice The old times were lovely. Hi, aloha! Come up, kiss patient-patient, the ladies, you know. And some men. Good friends, they hug each other. Beautiful. I can say old days people was beautiful.

Richard Marks
1930–2009

At the age of nineteen Richard was sent to Kalaupapa, where his father, brother, sister, and grandmother already resided. In the struggle for patients' rights, two men took up the banner most often: Bernard Punikai'a and Richard Marks. Richard also campaigned to make the settlement a National Historic Park, and traveled to Europe in the effort to first beatify, then canonize Father Damien. A former sheriff, he started Damien Tours, now operated by his wife, Gloria. He was not afraid to say he was a leper, using the word abhorred by many patients. With Damien's sainthood a sure thing, he renewed his passport to attend the ceremony in Rome, but died ten months before it, at the age of 79.

Richard The doctors told me I had leprosy, I figured it was the end of it for me. It was banishment, it was automatic in those days. And of course it was to Kalaupapa, the place the old Hawaiians used to call the living grave.

Pamela Were the sulfones already here?

Richard The drugs came into use when I came and I know how lucky I am because I saw what the disease could do.

Pamela Your appearance has not dramatically changed.

Richard People immediately recognize I have some kind of illness because of my features, my eyebrows are gone, my ears, nobody realizes what it is, but the way I was raised it was nothing to be ashamed of. Getting sick is no shame, no fault of your own. And people who are sick have most need for sympathy or family and friends around. The idea of being ashamed made it so bad for patients in the early days. Leprosy was about the most feared disease to hit Hawai'i, not because it did so much damage, but because you were separated from your families. This was because of the missionary influence. This was the first time the Hawaiians were made to face the concept of banishment. For one thing, they didn't understand contagious disease, didn't understand epidemics and Hawaiian families were close. As soon as somebody discovered you had it they could lock you up as a suspect up to a year. At one time the government was even paying a bounty on lepers, ten dollars a "catch."

Pamela On your settlement tours, how do you explain the settlement's creation?

Richard When the hospital, the receiving station in Honolulu, was full, they had to get rid of these people. They would charter a ship to bring them in from Honolulu. They would anchor offshore, put the patients in small boats and row them ashore and there were times when the patients were just dumped over the side of the ships. They had to swim to shore. There were some houses, temporary shelters, for maybe ten percent of the patients, but they just came down in the wind. Nothing could stop that wind. The conditions were so bad and of course there was never an adequate supply of food or anything else. The government sent administrators and everything else but nobody stayed. The doctors wouldn't come within twenty feet of a patient. There were Protestant ministers, Catholic priests, but nobody stayed. This is what made Damien special.

Pamela Kalaupapa became home.

Richard Those that survived came to love this place. Of course, most were crippled, disfigured. They had no idea, no desire to leave.

Pamela Is there a fear that the government will take the land and develop it for tourism?

Richard Yeah, there's plenty fear of the land being taken away from the patients. A lot of people have come to Kalaupapa over the years and they keep reminding us of what is happening all over Hawai'i. Development is Hawai'i's lifeblood, so we don't feel at ease. This is our own. We earned the right to stay here.

Pamela How would you like people to remember Kalaupapa?

Richard Remember it for what it was, a place of great loneliness and despair. Remember there are so many people in other parts of the world suffering from disease. This could be used as a perfect example of what a few devoted people like Damien can do to change things, no matter how horrible things are.

Jimmy and Nancy Brady
Residents of Hale Mōhalu, Kaimukī

At the time Jimmy was a guide for tourists visiting Kalaupapa. Nancy was a volunteer with the Police Department. Both came to the settlement as children. Their two children were born in Kalaupapa and relocated to Honolulu to live with Nancy's mother. After relocating to Hale Mōhalu, they took frequent vacations to Las Vegas.

Jimmy A lot of people was afraid of leprosy. If you had any discoloration other than the natural color of your skin, you was known to be like a suspect of the disease. In my situation I had a white spot on my arm and it was not a natural coloring, so I was taken as a suspect.

Pamela Who reported you?

Jimmy There was this district nurse in Honolulu. These were the nurses who went out looking for people who had the disease. Their attention was brought by my teacher in school.

Pamela Did you know you had the disease?

Jimmy No. I didn't even know what leprosy was. In 1941, I was taken from the family to be placed in this institution.

Nancy Kalaupapa was feared in those days. For me it was 1936. I was afraid. We felt once you came here there was no return. I would never return home. In those days we didn't have medications, those treatments to arrest the disease like we do today.

Pamela How old were you?

Nancy I was thirteen years old. I said goodbye to my parents. My mother was at the wharf. I am on the SS *Hawaii* and it was a really sad, sad day. Saying goodbye isn't easy, especially knowing you won't ever return to your family. And to me, this was to be my last goodbye to my father.

Jimmy I was deported on May 15, 1942. No one could see us from the wharf because we were kind of like in a chute, coming out like cattle into this deck of the ship, which was actually a cattle ship, and we was placed on this deck with mattresses on the floor and we could still smell the bad air from the cattle waste which was on the ship.

Pamela Was your family there to see you off?

Jimmy My family knew I was being deported but they didn't know when, so they was not there on the pier. Thinking back, I can truly say it was frightening. I remember one of the guys on the same ship. His mother was here in Kalaupapa. And he wanted so much to see his mother again. He asked me to go along to visit his mother. When we got there we both became so afraid because she was so badly disfigured. I really cannot express the feeling and the sight that I saw, so much of this woman was afflicted with leprosy. I look at my friend and he look at me and we was afraid because it was a horrible sight. He never expected to see his mother in that disfigurement. Somehow we got used to it. Then every time we had the opportunity to visit his mother, we became more relaxed, more accustomed to it, we had a much better feeling. But truly it was the most frightening sight I ever saw.

Pamela Did you keep in touch with your families?

Nancy With my mother I was always in contact with her, but when my brothers came down from topside, hiking the trail, both came down to see me, by then several years had gone by and I was changed in my physical appearance. I was shame. Even though they were my brothers. They accepted me and all we could do was cry together. To have your family waiting for you with open arms after twenty or some odd years, and having changed in my appearance, but still they accepted me and loved me as if I was never away from home.

Pamela After you gave birth, did you feel bitterness at not being able to care for your children?

Nancy No bitterness because I understood that upon giving birth I would never be permitted to touch them. This I understood. I knew they would be taken away from me, but every mother wants to touch their child, have their child close to them. This is what I missed. More than anything in my life I missed being with my babies, taking care of them, being a real mother to them, taking them to school and going to PTA meetings, going picnicking with them, these are the things I missed.

Pamela But the bond of love remains.

Nancy Yes, there is a strong bond of love that was really taught by my mother. She told them about us, their father and mother, and she taught them to recognize us as their parents and to love us and make them understand why we are separated, not of our choosing but because of the disease.

Pamela What does living in Kalaupapa mean to you now?

Jimmy When I first came I felt like an outcast of the world, like all our people felt. For the world to know, sure, we suffered a lot, but for the life I'm living, I thank God for this, because he gave me my wife. I know deep in my heart we lost the best part of our lives, our youth. But because of that we had to learn to make the best of it, make our own happy life. Now if they ask us to leave I don't feel that is right. Where will we go?

Nancy Living in Kalaupapa today I can tell you that I am truly happy. We've lived here almost forty-five years, I am really happy because we are surrounded by people who care for us, who take care of our needs. And today I am so grateful I have a good, loving husband, a nice home. We do things together, we have a family that loves us, and we have people around us who are like us.

Paul Harada
1925–2008

Paul Harada was climbing the rocks with a throw net when I first met him. Paul was born on Kaua'i. His diagnosis in 1945 was a surprise to the family, which had no prior history of the disease. Paul would later say he thanked

God for leprosy because it led him to the Catholic faith. In Kalaupapa he met and married Winnie Marks (Richard's sister), who now resides at Hale Mōhalu, Kaimukī.

Paul Fishing is the most popular activity because young and old can do it. People here really do enjoy fishing. They fish with nets, poles, anybody can fish. I still do a lot of fishing but whether I catch or not, doesn't matter. Well, yeah, it does matter, but we're conscious of exercise and running and I just enjoy myself running up and down these rocks.

Pamela As a child, did you know what leprosy was?

Paul I had an idea that it was the worst thing in the world. Better to be dead than have leprosy, right? Those days leprosy was known as the Moloka'i Sick. Everybody feared the disease, including myself.

Pamela Was Kalaupapa a prison to you?

Paul Not like a prison, worse than a prison. Prison at least eventually you go out. Kalaupapa in those days was depressing because many of us didn't expect to see our people back home. And each year you grow progressively worse. If you're, what they call, blossoming out, in other words you're showing ulcers, it's rapid. Most of it is the extremities, your hands, your face, it's just a mass of sores. I was just in the stage where within, I thought that between four and five years I would get so sick that I would be gone.

Pamela Did the drugs help you?

Paul The sulfones, in '46 was introduced in Hawai'i. On the Mainland it was used since '41. All of these ulcers and sores started to subside and within three months you became sort of human again. People here, even with all their handicaps and sufferings, have accepted their lives and basically they're a happy lot. There's a lot of misery at having no fingers, whatever, but they've accepted it and don't spend much time thinking about it. If I had to tell anybody, give a message, I would say, "Hey, whatever your problems may be, it's not as big as you think. You're not the only ones with problems. We have about the worst thing to have but then there's probably something worse out there." We have come to the conclusion, it's better to look forward to something better. Why dwell on what you don't have? It's already lost. It's senseless. Life isn't just having good hands or a beautiful face. Have a beautiful personality is something, too. It's what you are that's important.

Ben Pe'a
1896–1981

Ben had two constants in his life: cats and the Catholic faith. He was eighty-three and blind at the time of our first interview, but he walked confidently without assistance from St. Francis Church to his yard. He had been in the settlement since 1912. As an elder he felt it his duty to give me my Hawaiian name.

Ben I sing that concerning that what you call, raw fish. Do you eat raw fish?

Pamela Yes.

Ben And *'opihi*?

Pamela Yes.

Ben And *kālua* pig?

Pamela Of course.

Ben Oh, then you burn the town. I sing now?

Pamela Okay.

Ben I love all Hawaiian Islands
For the poi and raw fish
I love all Hawaiian Islands
The 50 state of America.

I love all Hawaiian Islands
For the poi and raw *'opihi*
I love all Hawaiian Islands
The 50 state of America
The 50 state of America.

The wind is blowing today
The sun is shining bright.
And the rain falls now and then
What will be, will be.

God the father made heaven and earth
And all that there is.

Pamela Did you write that song?

Ben No, not write. Just pick the words up and yak, that's all.

Pamela You like to sing?

Ben Well, make noise, yeah? 'Cause my company is cats. The cats like I make noise. You sing?

Pamela Only in the shower.

Ben What your father's name?

Pamela William Young.

Ben He Chinee?

Pamela Yes.

Ben And your mother, she Chinee too?

Pamela Yes. Her name is Grace.

Ben Do I know them?

Pamela I don't think so, unless you lived in Kalihi-Pālama.

Ben What your middle name?

Pamela It's Chinese. It means good moon.

Ben I have a better one. Momi is Hawaiian for pearl. That's your name.

Pamela Then I will be Momi.

INTERVIEW WITH YODIE "NOE" MIZUKAMI
Makia's niece

Noe When Auntie (Ann) was alive I was working with the both of them. She made it my job to look after Uncle (Makia). I've been doing that since 2006. What happened was Auntie went to my whole family and they couldn't handle her.

Pamela Why?

Noe She had to have her own way. And she was his advocate. Nothing goes with him unless it goes through her. So knowing she wasn't going to be around she was trying to groom me into being her. But it's different because I have a life. I tried to do my best to be on his medical directive. And because he's older than me, you know, Hawaiian style, automatically you respect. But the rest of the family, couldn't handle.

Pamela What was the problem?

Noe Auntie grew up in Connecticut in a privileged home, the family owned businesses. Well-to-do. They had maids and stuff. She didn't know how to make a bed. Educated, but when it came to life and common sense she didn't have it. She made tuna salad by putting the whole can in the bowl. She didn't know how to use the can opener. So she had to learn. So I would do it and she'd say, "Oh, thank you. You so smart!" And I'm thinking, "Oh, my God." She was kind of detached from her family by choice, comes to Hawai'i, teaches classes.

Pamela What was she teaching?

Noe Death and dying classes, because when she passed away she planned her own funeral. She even has Uncle's funeral planned. I was cleaning up and I said, "Look, Uncle, she wrote your eulogy." And he said, "What?" Auntie, she had some strange ways. I would tell her, "Auntie, if you going to piss me off I'm going to leave. 'Cause if I stick around it's going to turn ugly." But Uncle was always the buffer. He would say, "Noe, try to understand Auntie. She's my wife and I love her. She cannot help."

Pamela But she loved your uncle.

Noe She did love him and she took care of him and she made sure his needs were taken care of. She was the decision maker and she had no problem telling people where to go. She loved the Hawaiianness of people, but she could not be Hawaiian. She wouldn't know how to say things to people. She hired some people to help and they would call me, crying because she wasn't nice to them, she was demanding. And I would say, "Quit then." They would fall in love with Uncle but they had problems with her. But to know the man, you had to know the woman behind him.

Pamela She had a problem with a Kalaupapa book?

Noe They were working with this author on a book and they trusted, but when it came out some of Uncle's words were changed and she was livid. They called the publisher and threatened this and that. She didn't even like the title. It caused some bad feeling in the Kalaupapa community because the book involved a bunch of people and I think some of them thought Uncle and Auntie were a little too High Mucka-muck for them. It wasn't that. She just didn't want his words changed.

Pamela She took on the task of preserving his work?

Noe Everything is on computer disk, yet when I read some of the stuff to Uncle he said, "Wow, that doesn't sound like something I would say. I wonder if she changed it." And I said, "I don't know, I neva' see her change it."

Pamela How did you find out she was sick?

Noe She had some kind of knee injury. Uncle was in Kalaupapa and he asked me to check on her. I took her to the hospital and did all the tests and she had low blood. The results came back and she had cervical cancer. On her deathbed, she had me calling on the phone, trying to, you know, Hawaiian tradition, asking forgiveness of people, trying to tie up loose ends.

Pamela What was the funeral like?

Noe They had a circle of friends and what they did is get together at that church up by UH, the Crossroads. I got the room and the food and we had a memorial service where people would come up and speak. She wrote a love letter to Uncle, which I read. Then we took the ashes a week later to Waiʻanae. That was her wishes. Out on the boat Uncle chanted, that was her wish, too. She wanted everything just so. She bought this blanket thing and the box. It had to be biodegradable. It had to be, she said.

Pamela What do you know about the Malo family curse?

Noe I know the story but I never thought of it as a curse. It wasn't explained to me that way. I just knew my Grandma was possessed and my Grandpa was hired by the family to take care of her and then they got married. But it wasn't talked about because we're a Mormon family and we ate, drank, lived Mormon. But actually, wow, that's right. My Dad had the only son, my brother George Jr. He has three sons and three daughters and they have children, all daughters. Wow, that's right, no more boys.

Pamela How proud are you of your uncle?

Noe So proud. For him to go through all he's been through. For the family to endure so much. They are a part of history. ◆

The Poetry of Makia Malo

TARO

In the early morning,
      a bouquet of winds swirls above the *loʻikalo*;
      a cold wind sweeps down from the mountain,
      a rush of fragrant ginger;
A seawind crowds the shore,
      invading the land with the pungent odor of *līpoa*.
I walk along the *ʻauwai*,
      the *ʻauwai* that flows among the *loʻikalo*,
      the strong smell of wet raw earth surrounds me …
As I move on;
      this is a gentle walk.
I pause, then touch the water with my toe;
The water is painfully cold.
I shiver, burrr …
This is a hurting walk!

I must not hesitate, yet I do;
I must be bold if I am to overcome,
      still I don't …
Then I think of all the work that must be done;
Weeds that need attention,
      two rows of taro to be pulled,
      their beds rebuilt, new suli planted …
I take a deep breath, then take the hurting walk!

THE IMU

Papa calls, "Come help with the *imu*!"
After we *hemo* the dirt,
      take out all the rock from in there.
I bend to the task,
      and work alongside George again
      as Papa supervises.
No need to supervise!!
The imu is cleared of all *'ōpala*;
Cut *kiawe* is placed in the *lua* just so;
Porous *imu* stones cover every log.
A long-handled shovel stands upright
      at the very center of the woodpile.
Then I am ordered to pour kerosene
      into the hollow once the shovel is removed
No need to order …
Papa lights the match, and tosses it in the center.
Fire meets paper, kindling soaked with kerosene.
Smoke curls upward tenuously through rock and wood,
      soon, flames!

The *imu* blazes as George and I keep watch;
There is a need to keep watch!!
Papa goes home.
The screen door slams shut behind him,
      his hard work all *pau*!!

DREAM TIME

'Twas in that dream time
Between deep sleep and awakening
When the trill insinuated itself into my dream, it's so beautiful!
I have to know what kind of bird makes that particular sound.

I've got to know where it is.

"Where," I thought, "is this strange sound coming from?"
I looked everywhere.
Up the mountainside
To the trees on the left and the right
The fear made me to tremble.
I could not understand
Where this sound came from.

I blinked.
And still "There it is again.
It's repeating itself.
The same trill
And it seemed to be getting louder
And louder."
I stretched out my arm and touched
        the top of the tallest tree.
Surely as tall as I am
I can see
The bird.

Yes, it must be a bird.
"Where is it?"
Fear began to take hold and I trembled.
I waited for the next trill.
Now the trill is softer and lighter
As if it's leaving me.
As if it came to be with me.
And now I am sad
I no longer hear it
Will we meet again the next dream time?

BANANAS

We were seven
An insignificant seven.
We lived at Hale Mōhalu
On the other side of Heaven.
We were little bit *kolohe*
But never really mean.
We only stole bananas.

Always ripe—no, never green.
We stole them by the bunches
In the dark of night it was.
Creeping dried leaves went crunches
And the alarm went abuzzzz.
Wha dat? we whisper, oh, so loudly
We scared. We laugh.

And then I tell 'em proudly
Das only my oversize feet
As I beat one hasty retreat.

KATIE'S STORE

I walk past Katie's Store on my way to the hospital.
The dark yawning inside the open door intrigues me, but I hurry past.
      I have no money.
Yet I know beyond the door, past the dark,
Get all my favorites—ice cream … soda … candy …

Suddenly, I see a face;
An almost featureless face;
A face whose eyes show the discoloration of one blind;
A face whose nose has been ravaged, flattened;

And the skin—
Mottled with so many scars from all those sores over all those years
        that festered, then healed;
Mouth misshapen;
Lips and ears eaten away.

Then it smiles:
A grotesque smile.
        I quiver.
Tears flow because I'm afraid.
Never have I seen anything so scary.

I am a boy of twelve
And not prepared.
Pili, my kid brother, didn't warn me:
Beka, my sister,
And certainly Pu'a my oldest brother couldn't have.
How could they?
They forgot what it was like
        The first time.
I cry more tears,
But in spite of all the tears,
Somehow I sense more than know,
That the smile is not to torment.

Then I feel shame;
        So ashamed.
For Mama taught me always to be kind, to respect. "No make fun!
No make sassy and stare!"
But all these teachings give in so easily to fear.

Through the tears I look again.
        This time,
A swollen, fingerless hand
Reaches out.

Waves,
And bids me enter.

"Come, boy."
Sound like that coming out of a grave calling.
"Come. No scared.
I like aloha you and treat you to something.
Eat ice cream, drink soda—how 'bout candy? You like candy?
Come. No scared."

More tears flow,
More I shake,
Startled by his ghostly voice,
My eyes locked onto his disfigured hand.
He knew that I was scared,
But patiently,
He *ho'omalimali* me;
His voice kinder, softer.

"I know, boy. I ugly.
I stay all bus' up.
I wish I can look nice so you no scared me, but no can help.
I look how I look.
So, boy, if you can forgive how I look,
I like buy you something.

"You know,
First time I come this place, Kalaupapa, I look jelike you;
        face clean—no scars, nothing; body, felt—good! Strong!
Still young yet.
Hands? Eh—only one side little bit *pehu*. You know, swollen?
Before, me, I like sing—*kani ka pila*, play 'ukulele, guitar,
But nowdays I jus' come Katie's Store, drink beer.
If I stay home, only listen radio alone.
Too lonely, dat!

So I think, mo betta I come Katie's Store.

"So, boy. Come. Come. Come ova' hea.
Sit by the table.
Katie! Katie! Bring ice cream, soda, candy for the boy."

My legs move,
And soon I'm sitting at the table,
My cravings for the sweets
Stronger than the fear.
In time I learned to respect this man.
In time I learned to love this man.
And now I'm doing my damndest
To bring honor not only to him,
But to others like us.

HOPSCOTCH

Safety pins and bobby pins
And *ina* for hopscotch,
A magic kiss in hopes that this will land 'em on the mark
Hissing, boos, cheering, delight. "Come on. Come on,
        you bugga!"
To coax and aid it on its flight.
We hop and skip and leap and jump
From here … to there … to there.
With arms flailing,
Torso twisting,
All a-listing,
On one foot,
All our weight to bear.
A balancing act
While bending, stooping
One hand racing,

Fingers creeping, inching forward slowly
To snare the *ina*
Of safety pins and bobby pins
For hopscotch.
We stand aside, as players do,
And wait for one mistake.
We squeeze *'ōkole* and we beg,
"Oh, please! Don't make it! Pleeeeze!!"
With fingers crossed
Our jinx we toss
And jeer to shake her up.
We hope she thinks our curse is strong
So that she falls—kerplop.
While stretching, always reaching
For her *ina*
Of safety pins and bobby pins
For kids who play hopscotch.

DAMIEN

You are the wind that came and swept across this land.
Your cool breeze eased the suffering, overcoming the heated sickness,
        keeping it from overwhelming us and bringing sweet relief.
You are the waves that come from across the ocean,
        touching our shores, each wave a gentle touch, restoring faith
        and love and hope so we could continue to live and dream.

The aftermath of your waves leaves your imprint upon the sands of
        time marking forever your place as one beloved, one
        unforgettable, one who walks with God—and us, forever.
The rains come like the tears that flow from our eyes as we weep for
        those—our beloved *'ohana* who went before us, who raise
        their hands in acknowledgment of you,
Ē Kamiana!

We thank you for your commitment to your God,
     to your fellow man that you gave your life
     to bear the dreaded disease,
     the filth of pestilence and the shame and dishonor
     heaped on us in our lonely exile by our fellow man.
You are the one committed to ease pain and suffering,
     bearing all upon your shoulders.
We raise our eyes and our voices up to the heavens
     and implore the gods to walk hand in hand with you
     as you walked hand in hand with us
     and the suffering during this lifetime.

You are the love, *Ē Kamiana,*
     that holds us together in the land of the cool breezes.
The rains that weep upon the *pali,*
     the sun that warms the land of Kalawao,
'Oia, ho'i, Ō Kalaupapa.
Aloha Ē. Aloha Ē. Aloha mau loa Ē.

You stood alone, high above man,
     high above the land, forgotten at one time,
     left to rot and decay.
Undaunted, you forged your way through obstacles set in your
     path by many.
Today, your devotion gleams like a beacon.
It inspires others to tread in your footsteps.
Aspirations come to many, but for only a few are dreams fulfilled.
The path is long and lonely and very difficult.
     Only the strong love for one's God gives the strength
     to persevere, inspires love to overcome fear.
And the countless things needing to be done,
     most often without thanks,
     without acknowledgment, without fanfare.
There is no need to crawl on the ground,

to wallow in the *haumia* of despair to hide one's face,
    to wear a cloak of shame.
Stand tall!

With a loud voice proclaim the name and the love of God.
Ask that He grant us the will to continue bearing
        the torch that will light the path for many.
We are the descendants of those whose pain and suffering
        you eased.
We are the descendants of those who died
        with your care and the love of God in their hearts.
We are the descendants of those people to whom you gave shelter,
        spiritual comfort
        and whose hand and voice were the last to give benediction.
Ē Kamiana Ē. Ē Kamiana Ē. Ē Kamiana Ē. 'O 'oe na! Kai aloha ia.

BALDWIN HOME

In the late afternoon
Baldwin Home lies deep in the shadows of the *pali*
So picturesque against the muted hues
Of the steep, sheer mountainside.
The sun has begun its downward journey
Smudging any harshness from view.
The wind blows soft
And only slight movements
Can be detected among the trees' rich foliage.
Several coco palms rise
High above the grounds,
Like candles on a birthday cake;
The gentle swaying of fronds,
Like flames of emerald green,
flickering brightly o'er the lush grounds … beacons!

The white stone walls that guarded
Both sides of the entrance
Looked as solid and stoic
As the *pali* itself.
Each stone stuccoed in place
Visibly outlined.
The extra-wide front porch of the main building
Tumbled down the stairway
To where dwarf palms
Pushed out their broad fan-shaped fronds
Like foot guards braced against intruders
Standing on each side
Of the graveled path.

Its roof and those of the outlying cottages
Giving it the air of an alpine chalet
With only the tropical setting
To remind you it was not.
From here, soft rumblings of surf
From the distant black sand beach that lay below the switchback trail
Sometimes were heard like one's murmurings in sleep.

Chiming vespers from the little chapel
Float on the evening air
Their lonely, mellow tones welcoming twilight.
Voices that once echoed through the halls
Are long gone.
And the Brothers
Who cared for them
Are no longer here.
Baldwin Home, too, is gone
And lies still and quiet in the past.
But never forgotten.
Never.
God, it was so beautiful.

THE BIRDS

Another morning begins for me.
In the pre-dawn, I listen, where are the birds?
I have not heard the birds these past few mornings.
Instead, again I hear the roar, the tumultuous crashing of waves,
       huge mountains of water roiling in their death throes,
       hurtling themselves wave after wave,
       onto the brutal rocky coast,
       their thundering death cries rising and falling
       in the eternal struggle between land and sea …
But no birds.

One after the other, the waves come,
       committing themselves to their own total destruction,
       splashing and spraying foam in their aftermath.
An expulsion of bubbles forces an explosive "whoosh!"
       after each curling finish,
       becomes a dying groan.
The pauses between are never long.
They are relentless, the waves,
       with only one end, attack! attack! attack!
All else is quiet, early morning silent at Bayview, across the way,
       except for the reverberation of the booming waves
       between the buildings.
No doors slamming, nor pots and pans rattling yet,
       nor murmurings of sleepy morning voices,
       only a dog's muted bark somewhere far off.

I love these times … but still no birds!
The morning yawns and stretches into awakeness.
The day begins, and the air is heavy with a salty mist.
With the coming of light,
       all the night sounds have run for cover.
The day is overcast, and there is only a golden glow to the sun.

Though the scene at Bayview is tranquil, I can feel the
vibrations of the powerful surf on the rocks.
Each crashing sound shakes the walls of my bedroom,
especially if it breaks near the river's mouth
where there is a cave.
Then, even the ground above the lava tube shakes.
Time seems to hang still, the tableau before me indelible
in my mind.
The wind is squandering its energy somewhere else,
so the scene before me changes hardly at all,
and very slowly when it does.
The day passes uneventful, and time continues to sleep.
Yet the birds still have not sounded their presence.
Hmmmm! I wonder where could they have gone?

Later on, I notice someone walking along the porch.
He is surely taking his own sweet time to get to where
he needs to be.
How strange!
It's as if the ever present mist is muffling all sounds
strangling the very life out of existence.
Maybe that's why I haven't heard the birds!
The afternoon has brought some relief from the enveloping mist,
for the winds have breezed by in an irresponsible fashion,
heedless, even recklessly, routing the shrouding mist away.
The air is clear now, and I can hear the sounds of life everywhere,
the rustlings of leaves and trees,
the metallic creaking of car springs in protest, slamming doors.
But the most intrusive sound, of course, is the raging surf.

Now it is evening
It is as if the day is reversing itself;
those who are awake, now prepare to sleep.
Cars, rattling and squeaking, pass slowly in front of the house
now and then.

The air is still
All sounds are stilled, except for the waves
They pound! and pound! and pound!
They have been casting themselves onto the rocks below all day long.
Still later, the night has grown chilly.
The wind has picked up, and the long glass panes loosened
        from weathering, rattle ceaselessly in their age-worn
        wood frames.
The wind whips through the screens;
The chill envelops me,
        it is penetrating … hands and feet are cold!
The sea is angrier now, and the crashes resound ever louder.
An unease begins to take hold as I sit in my cottage by the ocean,
        a blanket held tightly about me.
The chair scuffs the floor as I rise to close the windows against the cold.
Maybe tomorrow?? The birds??

GUAVA MAN

The guava man came,
An empty 'eke huluhulu draped over his shoulder.
He was tall, spare,
Short tufts of white hair poked out
From under his floppy hat
That shaded a real craggy face.
His eyes were kind.
With a meerschaum pipe gripped firmly in his teeth,
And his gnarled walking stick, he moved in a cloud of tobacco smoke.

We had seen him
As he walked across the Papakōlea bridge.
"Eh! The guava man hea!! The guava man hea!!"
Echoed down the lane.
The message spread, and soon

Voices attached to little brown children
Were everywhere, surrounding this giant
As Lilliputians around Gulliver.

"If we go help you pick guava,
You pay us?"
"Yes, of course,
But can't use all of you. Sorry.
Don't have enough money to pay all of you.
Need a few good workers though.
Maybe four?"

"Me, Mistah! Me, Mistah!"
Hands raised, fingering the air,
Eager eyes searching the wrinkled face.
He was familiar to us, this guava man.
He'd been here before.

"Okay. You, you, you, and—you."
Others watched, as the lucky four
Ran ahead of the *haole*,
To where the pungent smell of ripened guava
Hung heavy in the air.

Summer was high season.
The trees were low,
Fruits easy to pluck,
And I picked plenty!
"One for the *haole*, one for me.
One for the *haole*, one for me."
Chins and tee shirts stained,
Breath sweetened with guava,
With hands thrust forward,
We returned to the *haole* in triumph.
I was lucky.

I earned fifteen cents that day,
For half an hour,
Picking guava …

TREE

There's a tree standing in Hawai'i still, ancient, tall, erect;
    with branches spread over ground open to the sun;
    branches spare of leaves save two.
The tree has withstood the years of weathering with grace;
    through its growing stages …
    seedling, sapling, postling, full maturity.
    then, the season of renewal, of promise … of life!
    the tree has come full circle,
For the blossoms scent the air,
    and soon, new seeds to propagate, and the cycle begins anew.
The tree has scattered its fruits;
Ti pits reseed the land.

Once in a long ago time during its youthful lushness,
Thunder clapped overhead
Lightning split the tree to its base
The tree drew strength from sun, wind, rain
Though divided, breathed as one
The land Hawai'i, nourished the struggling tree
'Onipa'a!

As wind rushed through branches
Leaves rustled in unison.
Rain quenched, the sun warmed.
Unable to flourish again, though tall and erect now awaits its end
There is a tree standing in Hawai'i still
And when the last two leaves fall
So will pass another generation of 'ohana.

KA PALI

When I was young, and on an island,
The world about me was real … breathing … so alive
And I loved to stand at the edge of a low bluff at Kalawao,
      peering out to sea,
      and feeling the wind, *Kamoaʻe*, blowing against me.
I suspect it is *Kamoaʻe*,
For though I can't see her,
I can feel her
      for *Kamoaʻe*, the wind, is like a cat, playful, skittish;
      dependent, yet callously independent;
      attentive one moment, ignoring you completely the next;
So, I have seen her cat-footing her way upon the crests of waves
      from way out there, across the ocean,
      dashing between the islet, ʻŌkala
      and the ridge that juts out into the deep, and *ka lae o* Pāpio.
She gusts at me, as is her style till she buffets the *pali* directly below.
Then I feel her creep up over the edge, and rush past me;
      cooling my brow,
      and tousling my hair as she does so.

I know it is *Kamoaʻe*, for everyone knows,
      that *Kamoaʻe* bears the *hauna* of the ocean;
And in her wake, sends waves crashing onto the rocky shore.
      All along the shoreline, white foam, *ʻehukai*,
      splashes among the rocks, splatters high up the sides
      of huge boulders
      and agitates close to land.
The sea, *kekai*, is not rough today, just a wee bit feisty,
      so that from where I stand,
      the distant sounds of the crashing waves are muffled;
      like muted murmurings … soft, and low.
My gaze next follows the waves that reach almost to the base of a *pali*,
      before breaking,

and travels up the sheer cliffs before me,
   its face weather-scarred, and timeworn,
   and marvels at the grandeur of this *pali*
   standing between Waikolu and Waileia,
   loftier, majestic, towering even higher above me.
Shrieks filling the air come from *manu koaʻe*,
   swirling in tight circles inside the wind.
They leap off of the scarred face
   they soar high up in the sky, floating on the breeze,
   their cries faint in the distance.
Many shades of green-browns, specks of yellows,
   dark blues and gray nearly black,
   like curtains, drape the steep walls of the valley,
   from its highest jagged point to the tree-filled valley floor.
Kukui nut trees shimmer their silvery gray-green
   as *Kamoaʻe* flails among their branches;
   and the swirling hues mark her movements.
The sun is warm, and comforting.
Many times have I stood there … right there,
   at the edge, looking, just looking …
   and admiring all the beauty that lay about me …
   the land, the sea …
   the sky, a powder blue,
   with constantly shifting, puffy white clouds streaming by.
And *manu koaʻe* still a tiny white speck whirling up there;
And *Kamoaʻe*, the wind, still keeps *koaʻe* aloft,
   cooling the land, and soothing me.
My heart overflows with *pili aloha* for this small corner,
   on this one island.
My love reaches out, and takes root;
It takes hold … deep, deep into the heart … the soul …
The very essence of this land.
When I was young on an island, I breathed as one with the land.

TIME

My hands are tied
Do you want seconds of what you just ate?
Do you have the time to watch me take a turn around?
You have a minute to spare.
My hands will sweep across my face, since I don't give
       a tick-tock's damn.
Hey, I want one, too.
The buzz
Before time runs out.

Just a sec—give me a hand.
Did you wash your hands and face before you ate?
Don't be alarmed.
I'm in the numbers racket this time
       and I keep running around and around and around.
Oops, sorry. Wrong number. Don't be alarmed.
I'm running out of time 'cause I ticked
when I should have tocked.
What did the short hand say to the long hand?
On that last go around you were seconds ahead.

Question: How can you tell when it's wintertime?
Answer: The alarm goes brrrrrring.
What did the hourglass say to the clock?
Give me a hand, I'm running out of sand.
And you know what the grandfather clock echoed?
       Tick. Tock. Tick. Tock.
Every second sounds—1, 2, 3, 4, 5—and they don't use
       their hands either!
—And can you imagine, without any fingers, as well!
Time stood still.

NIGHT SOUNDS

In the darkening night,
I sit on a cold stone wall
Under this familiar old banyan tree,
Her sheltering branches
Hover protectively,
Spreading high above me,
Making me feel safe, nurtured,
And most of all, inconspicuous.

The evening is quiet,
The breezes are stilled,
The air—cool.

I'm comfortable here, cloaked in darkness.
No curious, prying, sometimes even smirking eyes
Watching me struggle,
Observing every move I make,
Even as I arrived at this spot,
Earlier this evening.

It is also quiet enough now,
To let my thoughts wander where they will.
Many crowd my mind.
They keep turning over and over,
Like pages being flipped by the wind
In an open book.
Dispassionately,
I observe my inability to focus
On any one thought.

Then a persistent sound intrudes upon them,
Interfering with my concentration,
Distracting me;

It keeps tugging at my mind,
And pulling it away from its woolgathering,
Forcing me to refocus my attention.

I soon realize what it is.
It's the sounds of traffic
From the newly opened freeway,
Echoing from across the distance
In a steady "sweesh."
I listen real hard, and I think,
"Wow! Just like waves …
Just like the steady rush of waves!"

Now and then an unsyncopated
Whump! Whump! Whump! WhumpWhump!
Destroys the steady swoosh of the surf-like flow of traffic.
An obvious discord—
An impudent clunker of a truck
Going clankety clank clank!
Rattles past,
Then fades off and away.

I try to push my ear all the way over there,
So my whole being can lock in on the sounds of the traffic!

Man, this is crazy!
Before, when I could still see,
I couldn't stand it when I just sat and watched the traffic,
The endless flow of traffic rushing past,
Hurrying off to somewhere.

Sometimes there'd be a bunch of us guys
Sitting on the eaves of the men's building,
Our eyes scanning all the traffic passing in review.
We'd laugh and cheer on a clunker

Smoking past,
Or "ooh" and "aah" the classic cars,
Or wonder—

But often, minutes would pass
Before anyone said anything,
Each of us locked in on our own thoughts,
For as we gazed at this parade
Of hundreds of cars streaming by,
The footlights of the stage setting,
For us, was an eight-foot-high chain-link fence.

Sometimes it was difficult—
I had a hard time handling the envy, the yearning,
The longing to be one of those people,
One of those nameless, faceless people
In one of those cars
Racing along Kamehameha Highway,
Going who knows where?
Just going.
Places to go, appointments to keep, things to do …
Racing away.

Instead, we were guests,
Hostages in this real drama,
Watching life
Pass us by.

 I sit in the dark under the banyan tree
And must content myself with enjoying sound,
Trying to embrace all kinds of sounds to enhance my world.

I sit in the dark,
Under this tree,
Feeling cold and lonely,

Trying to liken the rush of traffic passing by,
To the rush of surf upon a beach.

NIGHTWALK

Night seemed like a safe time to begin,
So, after the guard made his rounds at midnight,
After the nurse did her last bed check
 I stood just inside of the open door to my room, and listened!
The hallway and all lay quiet,
Then I stepped stealthily out of my room,
Groped along the wall to the end of the corridor,
Then worked my way right on out of the building,
My cane tap! tap! tapping
Along a path that was once familiar,
Oh, so very familiar!!!
But no longer!!!

Now, paths are strewn with so many obstacles
That were never there before.
My steps were hesitant at first,
Even reluctant,
Yet I had to go venturing,
For how else would I get there if I didn't start?
—Didn't even try?

Resolve stiffened my spine,
As a tiny voice
Echoed and reechoed in my mind,
Gently reassuring me, while fostering determination.
"You can! You can!"

Unwittingly, though, I couldn't help but call upon
        a skill no longer dependable,

As sightless eyes strained to peer through the dark,
Ears focused before me,
Every sense ranging the way, probing the darkness ahead—
Fearful of being hurt,
I kept a protective hand in front of my face,
To ward off impending danger.
The other firmly clutched the crook of the cane,
And maneuvered it clumsily from side to side,
Stabbing tentatively at the floor.

The tapping penetrated the stillness of the hallway as I inched ahead,
Each foot sliding cautiously forward,
As pawns advancing across the chessboard,
One pace at a time.

Nevertheless, the pressure weighed heavy as I crept on,
Trying to move as stealthily as possible,
The tension was constant, and the pressure, relentless.
Sweat beaded upon my brow, and spilled down my face
Soon I'm drenched, pj's soaked.
Cold, clammy.

And watch, as I groped about helplessly like one blind,
A mere klutz!
But what I dreaded more than having people see me struggle
Was to see me get lost, wandering about helplessly lost—
Then, finding it hilariously funny, laugh!
Then, to worsen matters—having to call for help!
Dammit! The very idea fills me with self-loathing!

With grim determination,
I returned my attention to the business at hand,
The sound changed when the wooden cane
Came into contact with the sidewalk.
Here, the surface is rougher

And I knew I was out of the building.
I pushed on, my senses on full alert!
I can feel the outdoors about me,
As I'm guided more by my memory at this point,
Than clues I can read to keep me safe.
I pause slightly, and sigh,
A wee bit of confidence strengthens my grip on the cane.
Careful step, after careful step.

Then, thunk.
My cane raps the iron railing of the bridge.
I heave a sigh.
Actually my breath escapes in an explosion!!
Suddenly, I'm aware of how my hand is trembling
And now, the cane feels more cumbersome, in my hand.
Yet I reached my goal
And no one saw me stumble.
I made it.
All twelve feet
From the door to here.
Who the hell said it was hard? ◆

The Stories of Makia Malo

THE SWEET POTATO THIEF

Owl was a farmer of Kohala, and every night he would work in his sweet potato patch, for the light of day hurt his eyes. He dug, he planted slips and in the drying times, he brought water to his growing vines. With pride and satisfaction, he saw potatoes pushing from the earth.

Then one night, he saw that some of his young potatoes had been pulled and eaten!! "Rat!!" he thought. "That dirty rat is too lazy and shiftless to make his own garden, so he comes to steal from mine. I shall keep a close watch out for him." Yet though he watched every night, Owl saw nothing of Rat. "He knows that I am watching, and so he must be doing his stealing somewhere else," Owl said at last.

Time passed. Owl saw his vines grow green and strong, with great potatoes pushing from the earth. "Oh, so many great potatoes," Owl said as he came out to harvest them. "I wonder if my storehouse can hold them all."

He seized a big potato top and pulled. Up it came … a potato top, but nothing more!! The marks of gnawing teeth showed what had happened. Owl pulled another potato top, and still another … and they were all the same. Rat had tunneled under the patch and eaten everything.

Sadly Owl filled his gourd with green potato tops. "One meal only," he grumbled, "maybe two … two meals at the most from my fine big garden."

He built a fire and heated stones. He washed and wrapped the pieces of potatoes, packed them in the *imu* with hot stones, covered the *imu* and then went about his other work.

"There is enough for two good meals," he thought as he uncovered the *imu* and sniffed the savory aroma of the roasted sweet potatoes. But there was little else besides the smell. Rat had come while Owl was away. He had uncovered the *imu*, taken all the food except a few scraps and carefully put back the covering.

"That wicked, wicked Rat," Owl muttered to himself as he ate a few scraps of potato and put the rest away. He thought, "I shall have just one more small meal tomorrow."

But when tomorrow came, the gourd was empty! Empty!! That thieving Rat had gnawed a hole and stolen the last bits of sweet potato.

For Owl, nothing was left except starvation. He grew weak and hollow-eyed—too weak to even hunt for roots and fern shoots. "Soon I shall die," he muttered dejectedly.

It was then that Hawk came to visit him. "What's the matter, Owl?" Hawk asked. "You look terrible! Are you sick?" "Yes, I am," Owl answered sadly. "Sick with hunger, for I have no more food left!" "Hunger?! I thought that you were a farmer!" Hawk cried in astonishment. "Farmers do not starve. They have gardens!" "I was! There was no better farmer in all of Kohala. I had a big patch of sweet potatoes, but who ate them all? Rat! That thief tunneled underground and chewed the bottom of every potato. Then he opened the *imu* and ate that. He gnawed a hole through my gourd bowl and took the very last scraps. Now, nothing is left for me but death."

"Why do you not get even and kill that thieving Rat?" Hawk demanded. "How can I now? I am so weak!" "Come along with me," said Hawk, "and I will do the killing. You will only have to help a little." His friend's words gave Owl new strength, so that he managed to limp along.

Rat saw them approach his hole and came out to welcome them. He thought that he was so clever that he stole without fear of getting caught, and he believed that Owl had never even suspected him. Before Rat could say aloha, Hawk pounced on him.

"No! No! Do not eat him!" Owl shouted. "Tear him into little pieces instead!" So Hawk tore rat into small pieces. And that is why rats today are small, and why they have no love for owls and hawks. But they are the same thieving rascals as that big Rat who ate Owl's sweet potato.

As for Owl, he is no longer a farmer, but a hunter, a killer of rats and mice.

SLEDDING ON PUNCHBOWL

Whenever we did something we did with, oh, big gang thirty, forty, fifty of us, we go *holoholo* way out mauka side, go up Tantalus, climb over the mountain, go to Mānoa, go get mountain apple or we go to Kapena. I have to tell you, when we used to go swim up at Kapena we had a real shaka game, you know, we used to ask each other and you supposed to ansa'.

"Eh, you like see the sunrise? And the sunset?"

"Yeah, I like see the sunrise and the sunset. Yeah!"

Well, as kids we swim naked, you see? So when dive, you go headfirst and you do one slow roll and just as your *'ōkole* come up you see the sunrise and when you go over you see the sunset. Ha!

The other thing, oh, we used to go out to Waikīkī, we no mo' money, we just do things where it didn't cost anything. Of course, on the way home we hungry, we passed somebody's yard, get nice kine mango, we go inside go borrow. We come back pay you back later on, yeah?

But the best thing I liked was going sledding up on Punchbowl. Hawaiians in the old days used to sled on what they call a *hōlua*, a long narrow board to slide on *pili* grass. In the old days they used to build the run out of stone and it would be shaped somewhat like da kine in the ski slopes, you know, what you call, a ski jump. But the Hawaiians, they put dirt and in between they put *pili* grass.

That's one of my fond memories of growing up at Papakōlea because Punchbowl had lot of *pili* grass, and the slope was so fabulous. You know, we didn't have that kine *hōlua* sleds. Ours made of wood that we borrow from people's picket fence when they not watching. Take 'em home, you know, cut 'em up, paint 'em up before the guy can claim his fence.

And then the other thing we needed was wax, and us enterprising youth from Papakōlea would go school, *aihue* color crayon, go home, wax up the bottom of the sled. But the other place we got wax from just below Papakōlea is this huge Chinese cemetery. Every spring, called Ching Ming season, da Chinese go to the cemetery to celebrate their ancestors and then they take all this food: lupchong, salt eggs, pork hash, beef tomato, sweet-sour ribs, you name it. And ah, I tell you, all the young people from Papakōlea to Mānoa, Beretania, Lusitania, Pacific Heights, 'Ālewa Heights, up by Nu'uanu side, Pauoa, they all come by the cemetery and they wait on the stone wall, all around the cemetery. And then, you see, when the Chinese get in their car and driving out, then all the young people closing the cemetery and we get one big bucket lū'au, man. Every grave we go pick up *kau kau*.*

"Eh, up that side get lupchong."

"Who like pork hash, this side."

Ho da *'ono*, man. But also what we get, these bright red candles left behind. And we'd keep those candles to wax our sleds.

One day I asked my kid brother Pili if he wanted to go sledding with me and my friends Baby Tano, Joe Boy, and Corned Beef. And of course Pili wouldn't pass it up. So the two of us grab our older brother George's sled and we rush up front, meet da other guys at the bridge, walk across da bridge, hit the road going into Punchbowl and we walk walk walk along da road and then we come to the last house and we start climbing all the way to the top.

Get little bit more hard for climb because you know, our *lū'au* feet, no more traction, yeah? *Pili* grass is so slippery that when you climbin' up, you step up one, you slide back two. Ah, just like we're doin' the hula. Den somebody say, "Eh, we go by da old run." We always call it the old run because no more grass already. In the past we use it so much we cause erosion, but ova' dere our *lū'au* feet digging in the dirt, you know, all the way to the top of the slope. Just as we reached the top the *lōlō* Corned Beef say, "Eh, we go try suicide hill." So all five of us walk across and now we standing at the top of suicide hill. We looking down, oh oh, we get little bit scared 'cause it's so high and so steep. Way at da bottom there's this stand of *haole koa* trees. What the older guys did, they go cut grass and pile up in front these big trees, so you know that when you gon' ride da sled you bang dat grass. But as we standing there we look, oh boy, we get scared because this is the first time us young kids were up there by ourselves.

We were about seven or eight, the oldest about eleven maybe and then we think, "What if we get hurt? Who gon' help us?" Just then that *lōlō* Corned Beef said, "Me first, me first!" He jump on top his sled and I push him off the hill. Ho, I can hear his sled going "whoosh" and dat thing is so fast, and then I hear Corned Beef going "Yeehaw" go down. Bang, he hit the grass so hard, Corned Beef's headfirst inside the bushes. We standin' out there, we watching him. You wanna make sure he still alive, yeah? We wait and then we see his leg kicking. He come out of the bushes, pick up his sled and he come back up.

Me number two *lōlō* so I jump on top my sled. My brother Pili and Baby Tano push me, but they push me so fast my sled shoot up in the air and "Wah!" I hang on my sled, then hit the slope and boy, that sled was so fast I remember hearing the grass, you know, the sound "shhh" underneath me. Every stone and every puka, when that sled hit, the sled shaking shaking shaking shaking. It tickle your *'ōkole*. You not sure if you *kūkae* in your pants or not. You see but you no more time fo' worry, because all of a sudden the pile grass is getting more close, and more big, and BANG, I hit so hard.

Instead of going into the grass like Corned Beef I went flying more high! And mo' far! Then the ground came up hit me and BANG, I was out cold. And then next thing I open my eye, look around. "Eh, how come? I stay underwater! How come I stay underwater?" And then my brother George shake me. He tell me, "Makia, you dang kid, wake up, you pissing the bed again." Aw shucks, I was only dreaming.

'OPIHI

I crouch upon the rock, my eyes fixed on the incoming waves. And I count, one, two, three. Then I rush, leaping from rock to rock, careful, trying not to slip; my *'opihi* knife, clenched firmly, scrapes the shells from their purchases. One, two, three, four.

My mind is counting rapidly, eyes on hands that work deftly, ears attuned to the rhythm of the waves to warn of their next rush to shore. To warn of their next rush to—to warn of their next as the foam peters away from around me, the rumble of the surging force reaches my ears, the next comber has already begun its approach. And I quicken my pace.

I continue scraping up to the last second. In my mind, I retrace my scramble back to safety. Even before I actually move, my mind has already scampered ahead, back up the plotted trail. I pant with the excitement of another challenge faced. The salty air assaults my senses, my eyes smarting from its sting.

The taste of salt is ever present on my tongue. The smell of raw *limu* and sea spray invigorates me. Foam has temporarily hidden the next rock on which my eyes have focused, searching, waiting until the dissipation of the white water as the waves pull back.

My eyes catfoot the next move. I wait until the waves have settled into their usual pattern before I begin to count again. As the waves have their pattern, so do I as I settle into mine. Attack, and retreat … attack, and retreat. The weight of all the *'opihi* in the bag around my waist impedes my easy scrambling. I search for a large flat rock high above the waterline on which I empty the contents of my bag.

'Opihi, an avalanche of *'opihi*, tumble onto the flat surface as the bag is turned inside out. Yet my hands remain busily prying *'opihi* as I continue to edge along the shore. But now, the tide is rising, and it is riskier to go on. I hoard my energy to cope with the cold, as the waves and winds have been constant, relentless, for the last hour.

I am shivering uncontrollably, and can't stop the shaking. My energy is sapped, heat reserves gone. I must search out and retrieve the *'opihi* before I can hide among the rocks to stay the wind.

The tide is running very high now. The sea's assault upon the rocky shore is taking a dangerous turn. The next surge thunders against the rock wall, crashing wave after wave of its pent-up fury, its rage ever increasing, endlessly spending its fury upon the land.

"Stop!" I shout in futility. "Enough already!" The echo of my voice is engulfed in the rush of wind that pushes the next thunderous comber toward land, and carries my cry and the spraying foam high above the escarpment in a final curtain that billows down to earth like little fluff balls.

I hear, and I smile. I return to my car to head home. I take a last look at the sea and say, *"Mahalo, ē ku'u pōki'i."* Thank you, oh my brother.

THE WAR YEARS

In 1943, my brother George and his friends made shoeboxes. You know, it's a small wooden box with a slant fo' you put your foot on while the guy polishes the shoe. All the boys had different areas downtown. It was after Pearl Harbor and there was military everywhere. My brother George says, "When Pilipili wakes up you guys come down Fort Street by the church, help out." So we went down Fort Street heading *makai*. When we came to Beretania Street George was there across the way. There's a doorway to a building and above that, on the second floor, was the USO. Servicemen all around the building from there all the way to Nu'uanu, all over the place.

"Makia, get customers for me," George says. So I walk down, pass the servicemen, I look their shoes.

"Shoeshine, Mac?" This one shakes his head.

"Shoeshine, Mac?" Maybe this time okay.

I don't know how much George charged but Pili and I got twenty-five cents for every customer we got for him. At the time it was only ten cents to go in the movie theater, the Hawaii, the Princess, the Roosevelt Theater. So George says, "Go movies, then come back and I'll treat you to lunch."

So we come back afterward to the restaurant on Fort Street and Nu'uanu. Oh, man, we really pig out: eggs, sausage, rice, chicken, bread, then waffles and pancakes. That's what I remember about those war years.

CEMETERY GARDENS

There are gardens in this place called Kalaupapa. Gardens of headstones and wooden crosses, sculpted pieces and crypts that lie like pages of an open ledger, whose accounts have never been measured in assets, just liabilities. One life per headstone; one life per cross.

Some of the gardens are clearly marked, enclosed by fences or the occasional low stone wall. There are many signs of those who were buried when the Homestead gave in to political expediency and the entire peninsula became both prison and haven for those with Hansen's disease. Then there are locations of earlier gardens overrun with thickets of Christmas berry, guava, and lantana. These were all but forgotten by the present-day folk. Awareness of them began only when cattle were being chased in and out of these hidden gardens, obvious signs of historic times.

For there are many more suspected places that embrace secreted ones. Signs of a substantial community during Damien's time lie hidden among the trees and lush overgrowth and there is no accounting for the number of those who have perished and disappeared. We are thankful that as we think of them the overgrown forest, foliage, and thick vegetation stand as a testament that they lived and died here. Their blood, their suffering, their souls enrich this land. Strange, though, that we who were separated from society, ostracized for fear of spreading the terrifying disease to others, were still separated within this place from those who took care of us. And stranger still that we were further separated from each other by the choice of religion we embraced. A Mormon in the Mormon cemetery. A Protestant in the Protestant cemetery. And a Catholic in their own as well. Though we became a kind of family by our years of seclusion, in death we were branded as our desires and beliefs guided us in life. But the land does not care. ✦

Chronology

1934 – October 10, Makia is born in Honolulu to Mary and William Malo
1940 – Brother Bill (Puʻa) is sent to Kalaupapa at age sixteen
1943 – Brother Earl (Pilipili) is sent to Kalaupapa at age seven
1945 – Sister Pearl (Beka) is sent to Kaluapapa at age twenty-three
1947 – Makia is diagnosed with leprosy and sent to Kalaupapa
       at age twelve
1949 – Makia and Pilipili relocate to Hale Mōhalu, Pearl City
1952 – Makia graduates from high school
1956 – Makia marries Ivy; they are divorced in 1961
1965 – Makia loses his vision
1970 – Makia enrolls at the University of Hawaiʻi
1972 – Makia marries Sharon;* they are divorced in 1975
1977 – Makia obtains a BA in Hawaiian studies
1989 – Makia takes vows with Ann; they are officially married in 1990
1994 – Makia and Ann attend Damien's pre-beatification celebration
       in Belgium
2008 – Ann dies of cervical cancer
2009 – Makia attends Damien's canonization at the Vatican

*The name of Makia's second wife has been changed to protect her
privacy.*

Mahalo

This book would not have been possible without the assistance of Yodie Noe Mizukami, niece and loving caretaker of Makia, and Sheldon Liu of Hale Mōhalu, who, as Makia's case worker, has also become his confidant and friend.

Mahalo also to the Hale Mōhalu staff and resident patients, who showed such great patience and understanding as we conducted interviews and conversations every week for nearly three years.

Our thanks to the State of Hawai'i Department of Health, especially Dr. Glenn Wasserman, and to fellow storyteller Jeff Gere, photographer Patrick Downes of the Diocese of Honolulu, and my husband, Gary Sprinkle.

And most of all, Makia and I have much *aloha* for George Engebretson and Dawn Sakamoto of Watermark Publishing, for providing the patients of Kalaupapa a venue for their voices.

Glossary

'aihue, steal
'āina, land
'eke huluhulu, gunnysack
'Ewa, area west of Honolulu
   (directional term)
auwē, alas
hanabata, phlegm
hānai, adopt
haole, Caucasian
haumia, defilement
hauna, stench
ho'omalimali, flatter, cajole
holoholo, run around
ina, marker
ka lae o, the headland
kāhili, feather standard
kahuna, priest, sorceror
kalakoa, many-colored
kālua, baked (traditionally, in an
   underground oven)
kani ka pila, play music
kau kau, food
kiawe, mesquite, algaroba
koa'e, tropicbird
kōkua, nonpatient helper
kolohe, mischievous
kukae, excreta
liliko'i, passion fruit

lōlō, stupid, feeble-minded
lua, hole
māhū, homosexual
makai, seaward
make, die
malo, loincloth
manu, bird
mauka, inland, toward the
   mountains
nīele, nosy
'ohana, family
oka, crumbs
'okole, buttocks
'onipa'a, steadfast
'ono, delicious
'o'opu, small freshwater fish
'ōpala, garbage
'opihi, limpets
pā'ina, feast
pali, cliffs
pau, finished
pilau, stink
pili aloha, loving friendship
poke'o, preadolescent
puka, hole
'uku, head louse
wahine, woman